BASIC FORMS
OF PROPHETIC SPEECH

Also by Claus Westermann

Prophetic Oracles of Salvation in the
Old Testament
Praise and Lament in the Psalms
Isaiah 40–66, A Commentary
(*Old Testament Library*)

BASIC FORMS
OF
PROPHETIC SPEECH

by Claus Westermann

Translated by Hugh Clayton White
Foreword by Gene M. Tucker

The Lutterworth Press
Cambridge

Westminster / John Knox Press
Louisville, Kentucky

Translation of *Grundformen prophetischer Rede,* Chr. Kaiser Verlag, Munich

Published in Great Britain 1991
The Lutterworth Press
P.O. Box 60
Cambridge CB1 2NT

Published in the United States 1991
Westminster / John Knox Press
100 Witherspoon Street
Louisville, KY 40202-1396

PRINTED IN THE UNITED STATES OF AMERICA
9 8 7 6 5 4 3 2 1

British Library Cataloguing-in-Publication Data

Westermann, Claus
   Basic forms of prophetic speech.
   I. Title II. [Grundformen prophetischer Rede]. *English*
   224.066

   ISBN 0-7188-2842-9

Library of Congress Cataloging-in-Publication Data

Westermann, Claus.
   [Grundformen prophetischer Rede. English]
   Basic forms of prophetic speech / by Claus Westermann ; translated by Hugh Clayton White.
       p.   cm.
   Translation of: Grundformen prophetischer Rede.
   Reprint, with new foreword. Philadelphia : Westminster Press, 1967.
   Includes bibliographical references.
   ISBN 0-664-25244-3

   1. Bible. O.T. Prophets—Criticism. Form.   I. Title.
BS1505.2.W413 1991
244'.0663—dc20   91-15207

Contents

Foreword

It is highly appropriate that this book should be reissued on the occasion of the publication of the English translation of its companion volume, *Prophetic Oracles of Salvation in the Old Testament*. Few works have played a more significant role in the modern discussion of the genres of prophetic speech—and consequently in the understanding of the role and message of the prophets—than Claus Westermann's *Grundformen prophetischer Rede*, originally published in 1960 and made available in English in 1967. In this work, Westermann set out what he saw as the characteristics of the prophetic judgment speech, arguing that its roots were in Israelite legal practice. Now that he has completed the circle by analyzing that other major type of prophetic address, the salvation oracle, it is important that each of these works provide the context for interpreting the other.

The first section of the book is a history of the investigation of the forms of prophetic address and of the oral and literary history of those forms. Westermann's account of the course of scholarship on these questions is selective, stressing those works that sought to understand the oral character of prophetic discourse and that contributed to the interpretation of prophetic speech in terms of a legal or juridical background. Certainly Westermann's most significant ancestor was Hermann Gunkel, who called attention to the oral prehistory of the prophetic literature and insisted that by analyzing the formal features of the literature one could relate the individual *Gattungen* (genres) to their life situations in the institutional life of ancient Israel. Westermann's works on the prophetic judgment speech and now on the salvation oracle have carried that program forward, specifically by applying Gunkel's questions to particular texts: Who speaks? to whom? What takes place in this speaking? With *Basic Forms of Prophetic Speech,* Westermann took the oral roots of prophetic literature for granted and attempted to recover—as did Gunkel—the original speeches, as delivered before they were collected and organized into books, and to identify the institutional settings from which the forms of expression had sprung.

If a consensus on the question of the particular forms of prophetic speech prevailed before the publication of this volume, it was Gunkel's view of the matter. He saw the negative side of the prophetic message expressed in two different genres, the threat (or threatening speech) and the reproach (or invective), which sometimes could be combined into a single address. Westermann demonstrated that this terminology was misleading. In the first place, viewing prophetic speech broadly, he argued that the function of the Israelite prophet was analogous to that of the messenger in the ancient Near East. Like the bearer of a letter, the prophet did not speak for himself but for the one who sent him, and like the messenger who read the letter to the addressee, the prophet spoke the words of the sender, in his case the words of Yahweh. The comprehensive genre for prophetic address was seen to be "messenger speech." This conclusion was based primarily upon the common appearance of the "messenger formula," "Thus says Yahweh," in the prophetic literature. This interpretation has been highly influential, but it has been challenged by Rendtorff on the grounds that the formula occurs not only with "messages" but also with a wide variety of other material, that messages do not always begin or end with the formula, and that there is such variability in content that the "message" cannot be considered a distinct genre.[1] But whether or not the prophet was fundamentally a messenger and his speech a message, Westermann called attention to an essential characteristic of prophecy in Israel, namely, that these individuals spoke on behalf of Yahweh.

Second, and more specifically, what Gunkel had called the threat and the reproach, Westermann identified as a single—and the most characteristic—prophetic speech, the announcement of judgment with reasons for that judgment. He distinguished between the speeches to individuals and those to the nation, taking the former to be the original form. The typical speech to the nation or the people as a whole includes reasons for judgment (an accusation and its development), the messenger formula ("therefore thus says the Lord") as transition to the second major part, the announcement of judgment, which—Westermann concluded—included the announcement of both the intervention of God and the results of that intervention. Westermann argued persuasively that "threat" or "threatening speech" is not sufficiently strong for what one normally finds in such prophetic addresses: They are neither warnings nor conditional threats nor predictions of the future but proclamations of what Yahweh plans to do. Moreover, it is clear that there are a great many texts in which the prophet, in announcing that negative future, drew a logical relationship between sin and punishment, communicating that the offenses of individuals or of the people as a whole were the reasons for Yahweh's direct intervention against them. Thus what Gunkel had called reproaches function as reasons for the announcement.

On one important point Westermann disagreed significantly with Gunkel. Gunkel, answering his first question concerning the speaker of the words, believed that the prophets distinguished rather clearly between their own words and the word of God. The "reproach"—in Wester-

xi

mann's terminology, the reasons for judgment—came from the prophet himself, based on his observations, while the "threat" concerning the future—in Westermann's words, the announcement of judgment—was revealed by God. In some individual speeches that seems to be the case, since the messenger formula stands before the announcement. However, that formula as well as the oracle formula, "a saying of Yahweh," can begin or conclude all kinds of prophetic words, including the accusation as well as the announcement. In short, there is no firm basis for concluding that the prophets clearly distinguished between revelation and their own observations.

Somewhat less convincing have been Westermann's conclusions about the roots of these forms of speech in Israelite institutions. He surmised that the judgment speech against the individual was the earlier form and that it was rooted in patterns of expression and ideas at home in juridical procedure. Consequently, he judged that the language of the basic form of prophetic speech was borrowed from the law court and should be characterized as the judgment speech. This probably claims more than the evidence will support. In reaching this conclusion about the juridical roots of the genre, Westermann depended heavily on accounts of prophetic activity in the books of Kings, accounts that certainly give us more information about the Deuteronomistic understanding of prophecy than they do about prophecy itself. It is better to be somewhat more neutral. We have attempted to modify Westermann's understanding with the category "announcement of punishment" to indicate that the pattern does not necessarily presume a formal juridical background. To call this genre a "prophecy of punishment" acknowledges Westermann's conclusions about its shape and purpose but does not link it so directly to a legal background.[2]

Klaus Koch's analysis of the prophetic genres presented a major challenge to that of Westermann. On the basis of his "act-consequence," or dynamistic, understanding of Israelite thought, Koch argued against both a juridical background and a legal pattern in the speeches. What Westermann and others called "announcements of judgment" he called, simply, "prophecies of disaster."[3] He alleged that the "prophecy" usually was formulated passively, thus reducing the sense of divine intervention to judge and to punish sinful actions. Rather, the acts were seen to set their consequences—disaster—into motion. He saw the prophecies to be rooted in the private oracles heard by the prophets. However, statistical analysis of the words of the eighth-century prophets shows that he was incorrect. Although passive formulations do occur, most of the announcements are expressed with active forms of the verbs and generally indicate the future. The identification of particular human actions as sinful and the drawing of logical connections between these actions and the announcement of punishment to be effected by Yahweh's intervention—these are typical patterns of prophetic speech and thought.

Several specific features of Westermann's work have been qualified or rejected on the basis of subsequent research. Concerning the pattern or structure of the prophetic speeches, his detailed outlines suggest more typicality than the evidence will support. There certainly are addresses that include all elements, and in the expected order: summons to hear, reasons for punishment, messenger formula, and announcement of judgment, including announcement of both Yahweh's intervention and the results of that intervention. But among all the prophetic addresses, the structure is quite variable, both in the order of these elements and in their number. What is consistent is the presentation of a communication from God announcing future events, commonly as punishment for the sins of individuals or of the people as a whole. Moreover, Westermann's interpretation of the so-called woe oracles in particular has been challenged. They are

xiii

not oracles—words from God—nor are they to be taken as somewhat specialized forms of the judgment speech. There has been considerable work on this genre since his book was published, and by no means has a consensus emerged. But it is clear that most of these speeches are not direct divine communications, nor do they concern the future, as an announcement of judgment or punishment does. Rather, they characterize their addressees in terms of their sinful or unwise behavior. Thus they are more like accusations or indictments than announcements.[4] Consequently, although a few of them are followed by such announcements, the announcement is not essential to the genre.

By no means can all the prophetic addresses be subsumed under a single category or two, such as announcements of judgment and of salvation—nor did Westermann say they could. He did, however, suggest that most of the forms of prophetic address had stemmed from this basic one. Since the original publication of this volume, many other genres of prophetic speech have been analyzed, some of them in detail. T. M. Raitt, Arvid Tångberg and others[5] have analyzed the addresses in which the prophets call for repentance or change. Hayes and Christensen have analyzed the oracles against the foreign nations.[6] There have been studies of the prophetic vocation reports and their vision reports,[7] and there have been numerous other works that have expanded our understanding of the complexity of the forms of prophetic speech and literature.

Westermann attempted to recover—as did Gunkel— the original speeches as delivered by the prophets before they were collected and eventually organized into books. That enterprise is important, but students of the prophetic literature are not as confident about the possibility of achieving that goal as they were thirty years ago. Most of them now recognize that conclusions about the oral level are hypothetical at best and highly speculative at worst. Nevertheless, the sort of investigation carried out by Westermann continues to bear fruit. The form critical analysis of the prophetic literature reveals individual units that make up that literature, the elements of the addresses and how they function in relationship to one another, and the aims or intentions of the individual units. Moreover, frequently one is granted a glimpse of the life situations that have shaped if not determined both the contents and the form of the literature.

GENE M. TUCKER

Notes

1. R. Rendtorff, "Botenformel und Botenspruch," *Zeitschrift für die alttestamentliche Wissenschaft* 74 (1962):165–177. Reprinted in *Gesammelte Studien zum Alten Testament* (Munich: Chr. Kaiser, 1975), 243–255.

2. Gene M. Tucker, "Prophetic Speech," *Interpretation* 32 (1978):31–45. Reprinted in *Interpreting the Prophets,* ed. James Luther Mays and Paul J. Achtemeier (Philadelphia: Fortress Press, 1987), 27–40.

3. Klaus Koch, *The Growth of the Biblical Tradition: The Form Critical Method.* Trans. S. M. Cupitt (New York: Charles Scribner's Sons, 1969); K. Koch, et al., *Amos: Untersucht mit den Methoden einer strukturalen Formgeschichte.* 3 parts. AOAT 30 (Kevelaer: Butzon & Bercker/Neukirchen-Vluyn: Neukirchener Verlag, 1976); Klaus Koch, *The Prophets.* Trans. Margaret Kohl (Philadelphia: Fortress Press, 1982).

4. See especially E. S. Gerstenberger, "The Woe Oracles of the Prophets," *Journal of Biblical Literature* 81 (1962):249–263; see also W. Janzen, *Mourning Cry and Woe Oracle.* BZAW 125 (Berlin: Walter de Gruyter, 1972).

5. Arvid Tångberg, *Die Prophetische Mahnrede: Form- und Traditionsgeschichtliche Studien zum prophetischen Umkehrruf.* FRLANT 143 (Göttingen: Vandenhoeck & Ruprecht, 1987); Thomas M. Raitt, "The Prophetic Summons to Repentance," *Zeitschrift für die alttestamentliche Wissenschaft* 83

6. John Haralson Hayes, "The Oracles Against the Nations in the Old Testament; Their Usage and Theological Importance." (Th.D. diss., Princeton Theological Seminary, 1964), and "The Usage of Oracles Against Foreign Nations in Ancient Israel," *Journal of Biblical Literature* 87 (1968):81–92; Duane L. Christensen, *Transformation of the War Oracle in Old Testament Prophecy.* HDR 3 (Missoula, Mont.: Scholars Press, 1975).

7. N. Habel, "The Form and Significance of the Call Narratives," *Zeitschrift für die alttestamentliche Wissenschaft* 77 (1965):297–323; B. O. Long, "Prophetic Call Traditions and Reports of Visions," *Zeitschrift für die alttestamentliche Wissenschaft* 84 (1972):494–500; B. O. Long, "Reports of Visions Among the Prophets," *Journal of Biblical Literature* 95 (1976):353–365.

(1971):30–49; Ludwig Markert, *Struktur und Bezeichnung des Scheltworts: Eine gattungskritische Studie anhand des Amosbuches.* BZAW (Berlin: Walter de Gruyter, 1977).

Translator's
Preface

The English-speaking student of the Old Testament is offered in this book a clear example of how the form-critical method may be thoroughly and consistently applied to the study of prophecy. This translation will help to meet that need. Though the major focus of the book is upon a single speech form—the announcement of judgment—the foundation is laid for a study of the whole of prophecy from this perspective. Furthermore, in the first part of the book, Professor Westermann has summarized and analyzed the works of the scholars over the last fifty years who have made major contributions to the development of the contemporary stage of prophetic research. This provides a valuable introduction to some of the major problems that have been, and still are, at the heart of the study of Old Testament prophecy.

The investigation presented here has required a change in some of the terminology normally used in the English discussion of prophetic literature. The German word *Wort,* used most frequently by Professor Westermann to refer to the basic prophetic message, is translated in most instances as "speech" or "utterance" rather than as the more common English term "oracle." This shift has been required by the fact that "oracle" must be used to translate the German *Orakel,* which Professor Westermann sometimes distinguishes from *Wort.* Because of the importance of terminological clarity in form criticism, it has seemed advisable in this and in other cases to

9

adhere closely to the German unless well-established English equivalents were available that did not conflict with the German.

Finally, I must express my genuine appreciation to all those who contributed to this work in its various phases: to Professor Westermann, who discussed problems with me as they arose; to the students at the University of Heidelberg; to Fräulein Hadumut Heurich and Fräulein Horstmann, who read large portions of the translation and gave substantial help with difficult passages; and to my wife, Ann, whose constant support and able assistance in each stage of the work has made the translation possible.

Hugh Clayton White

Tennessee Wesleyan College
Spring 1966

Preface
to the English Edition

The prophets of the Old Testament have exerted an influence far beyond the time in which they were sent by God with their message. The prophetic message by nature intends to awaken and arouse, to call the people of God back from their perverse ways. For this reason the prophetic message is closely related to the time in which it was proclaimed and for which it was intended; it is thus especially difficult to be able still to comprehend how this message was originally meant in a completely different world and in situations that have radically changed. The history of the investigation of prophecy shows how profoundly the understanding of prophetic utterances has changed in the course of the centuries. In the first part of my investigation I have given a few indications of the astonishing differences in the conceptions of prophecy in the history of its interpretation.

If one seeks the way to penetrate the real intention of the prophets, one possibility that presents itself is the linguistic form of the prophetic utterances which remains the same throughout the whole history of prophecy: it reveals that the prophets were commissioned to deliver a message. It will be shown that the resulting designation of prophetic utterances as messengers' speeches says not only something about their outer form but also something essential about their meaning and significance. If we begin with the understanding of the prophetic message held by the prophets and those who passed down

11

their words, we will also be in the safest position for inquiring into their meaning for our time.

In the investigation presented here not all prophetic utterances are examined, but only the judgment-speeches to individuals, those to Israel, and other forms related to them.

CLAUS WESTERMANN

Heidelberg, March 28, 1966

A. The History
of the Investigation

Until the eighteenth century, the prophetic books were handed down as self-evident and unbroken units in which no distinction had been made between the word of the prophet and the word of God. The prophetic book was equated with the word of the prophet which was, in turn, equated with the word of God. The research on prophecy, which began in the eighteenth century and came to flower in the nineteenth century, discovered a living man behind the prophetic book and heard the voice of this man through the book. The entire tradition found within a prophetic book was of interest only insofar as and inasmuch as it contained " genuine " words of the prophet. That which was not found to be genuine in this sense stood in a negative light. In a third period that is now beginning, both of the extremes — *only* God's word or *only* man's word — have reappeared with equal importance in an altered conception of tradition. This new understanding of tradition emphasizes that the word of God has come forth through a man, the prophet, and has been passed on by men; that the preservation, spread, and transmission of these words by those to whom they were directed — the hearers, the disciples, and those who were affected by them — is of no less vital significance than the utterance of this word; and that those who transmit the utterance play an important and necessary role in the origin of the tradition that is found in the completed prophetic books. These three factors together make

13

up the whole of a prophetic book. To begin by recognizing tradition as a third factor makes it possible to avoid both extremes. The research in recent times has thus been turned toward the prophetic tradition, and significant advances in understanding have been made in this area.[1]

In the meantime, the investigation into the forms and history of the prophetic speeches has passed too much into the background. There are still very few generally recognized fundamentals and conclusions. The following work will attempt to collect and evaluate the previous achievements and to show some basic lines for further investigation.

An attempt will be made below to show a few of the steps that have led only in recent years to the explicit inquiry into the prophetic speech forms.

1. *W. W. Baudissin,* Einleitung in die Bücher des AT *(1901)*

The point of departure is an " introduction " published about the turn of the century which is typical of the situation at that time. The second part of the discussion on the prophets deals with the prophetic books. The first chapter is " The Record of the Prophetic Word." Baudissin proceeds from the thesis which was then often reiterated: " The vocation of the prophet was the refined form of two kinds of vocation — the seer and the *nābî'*. Perhaps it was with Samuel that this deepening problem of the seers and *nᵉbî'îm* began " (p. 312).

He begins accordingly, with the preliterary prophets. His perception of the peculiarity of this preliterary prophecy is already very accurate: " proclamation of individual sayings, demands, threats, or promises which concerned individual situations. Actual speeches by Elijah are not reported." Following this comes an excellent characterization of this early prophecy: " His word breaks in like light-

14

ning from heaven igniting sultry air, and suddenly the
speaker is carried away by the spirit onto one of the mountains and one seeks him in vain " (p. 316) . Baudissin distinguished this early epoch of prophecy from the appearance
of prophets as orators which can be recognized with certainty only from the eighth century on. This rhetorical
form must have effected a change in the entire nature of
the prophetic work to follow: " It included a generalization which made it useful in other times and situations "
(p. 316) . Baudissin sees this as the reason for its fixation in
written form. Here, an especially instructive observation
follows. Baudissin notices that through this generalization,
" a moral-religious deepening " occurs: " Yet through the
fixation in writing, they ceased being what they should be
and were intended to be; i.e., that which was understood in
its original form as God's word now appears veiled in
human paraphrase and interpretation. The old prophetic
word has in fact, perished in and through this fixation in
writing" (pp. 316 f.) .

It is to be noted here that Baudissin has instinctively
perceived that the essential nature of the prophetic speech
actually comes to expression more clearly in the work of
the preliterary prophets than in the " rhetorical form " of
prophecy. This means that he has already suspected that
the short, independent prophetic saying is only meaningful and understandable as an oral utterance and that this
is its proper form (" single judgments, demands, threats, or
promises which were valid for individual situations ") . Unfortunately, the " rhetorical form of prophecy " is not defined any more precisely by Baudissin. Here he obviously
succumbed to the traditional conception that the determi-
native unit in the prophetic books was the longer speech
(comprising about one chapter) . This was the view that
Gunkel expressed in his article in *RGG*[1], " Latter Prophets ": " Then the prophets learned to compose *longer
speeches* which sometimes comprise a chapter. But such
speeches are also seldom . . . constructed from a clear

15

point of view, but rather consist mostly of a more or less loose agglomeration of sayings. Often no clear train of thought is presented . . ." (col. 1878, Vol. IV) .

Baudissin virtually equates the "rhetorical form of prophecy" with written prophecy. Here an obvious gap in his work appears and into this gap later investigators will enter. There must surely be a *distance* between the work of the prophets as speakers and its fixation in writing. It is not plausible that they should be one and the same. Baudissin, however, can already give valuable insight into the question that arises at this juncture. When Baudissin says that the word of God now appears "veiled in human paraphrase and interpretation," the question of the relation of the word of God to the word of man in prophetic speech arises. This will be taken up vigorously in the later investigation. With this, he has clearly shown the way to the precise formulation of the question concerning the actual sense in which the prophetic speech is the word of God. The work of investigating the prophetic speeches must yet take a circuitous route, however, before finding the way indicated here.

2. *C. Steuernagel, " Die Propheten,"* Lehrbuch der
Einleitung in das AT . . . (*Tübingen, 1912*) ,
Abschnitt II, pp. 457 ff.

Here we find an essentially different type of elucidation of prophetic speech. To clarify this difference a relevant section must be cited:

" The content of the prophetic activity is extraordinarily different in every case according to the individual character of the prophet and the occasions. The individual character of the prophet is the product of the prior development of religious and moral understanding, the ability of the prophet which in the final analysis is inward and personal, and the stimulation which exists in the history of

16

the times. The occasion of the speech determines the particular direction in which the prophet continually works out and develops his thoughts. . . . It is very possible that he contradicts himself, for he can observe a thing differently today from yesterday. In the final analysis, however, his utterances always stem from the same kind of thinking and are joined in a higher harmony."

This is quite unmistakably the language of an idealistically colored religious individualism. We are astonished today at the ease with which the prophet is described as a speaker who " works out and develops his thoughts " in a particular direction, and most important, one whose " utterances always stem from the same kind of thinking."

Once this basic conception is bracketed out, a more precise conception of the kinds of prophetic speech appears. Here, also, the whole relevant section must be cited:

" In general one can characterize the prophets as an embodiment of the folk conscience. They place the behavior of their contemporaries in the light of the divine judgment. Because it usually contradicts rather strongly the demands of Yahweh, they come to accuse the people, to hold up before them their unrighteousness, and to summon them to a basic conversion. In particular they preach repentance to the leading circles. . . . They summon the people to justice and righteousness, to humility and trust before Yahweh, to religious honesty. . . . If their warnings are ignored, as is almost always the case, they proclaim the impending judgment which is depicted differently according to the signs of the times. The repentance and judgment sermon has by far the broadest scope, but it is not the final word. The ultimate purpose of the judgment is to create a holy people conformed to God upon whom Yahweh can bestow his grace. At this point the prophets take up the national Messianic hope, but with certain distinctions. Salvation was to be imparted only to the people who were purified through the judgment. Also the picture of the Messiah and the eschatological time of salvation was

17

enriched through the addition of religious and moral characteristics. This salvation prophecy is not of primary importance with the older prophets, but from the latter prophets of the exile on, it gains in importance and becomes to some extent the predominant element. The thoughts of the prophets are not only directed, however, toward Israel but also encompass the heathen nations, for Yahweh is to them the God of the whole world."

This is in its own way a masterful summary of the prophetic activity as it was understood at that time. One encounters it in similar form a dozenfold in later literature, but nowhere so clearly and comprehensively in a single summary. From our point of view the following can be said:

1. Clearly, two major forms of prophetic speech emerge here: the accusation directed toward the prophet's own people and the announcement of the punishment. It should be especially maintained that here " the content of the prophetic activity " centers in both of these.

2. An important characteristic of this summary is the logical arrangement of the whole. It begins when the prophets place the behavior of their contemporaries in the light of the divine dictums. This has, for the most part, a negative outcome and the prophets come to accuse their people (this accusation, therefore, has a judgment made by the prophet as its presupposition). The accusation is then identical to the repentance sermon and amounts to a warning. If the warning is ignored, then they announce a punishment. The judgment sermon is not the final word, however. The people should be so changed by the sermon that Yahweh can again impart his grace. But salvation will be the lot only of those who are purified through judgment. This picture of a logical or conceptual order (indeed, the concern here is essentially with " the thoughts of the prophets ") is in itself very clear and each of his sections is verified by the text. But that which is questionable is the whole structure as such. It is indeed a purely intellectual

18

construct and stands nearer to the retrospective Deuteronomistic view of prophecy than to prophecy itself.

3. This construct becomes dangerous particularly at the point of making the accusation identical to the call to repentance. Steuernagel succumbs to a traditional view that has not been overcome down to this day, i.e., the prophets are preachers of repentance. That, however, is simply not correct. Or to put it more prudently: as a statement about the whole of prophecy, it is a dangerous and confusing generalization.[2] According to Steuernagel, the call to repentance is now expanded into the warning that is extensively developed. Thus it almost appears that the call to repentance and warning are standing in the middle of the prophetic sermon. That is not the case. Moreover, in this intellectual conception the accusation and announcement of judgment are widely separated from each other so that the judgment sermon is caused only by a sequential arrangement of accusation, call to repentance, and warning which allows the hearer to turn his back on the warning of the prophet. This obscures the fact that in a majority of the prophetic speeches the accusation and announcement of judgment constitute one speech. They come together to form a prophetic judgment-speech on the occasion when the announcement of judgment implied by the accusation is actually uttered. Though that appears to be so clear and abundantly verified by the facts at hand, the intellectual construct that is visible here in Steuernagel has nevertheless indirectly exercised a significant influence upon the further investigation of the prophetic speeches.

One can cite a definite group of texts as one possible basis for this position. There is a group of speeches in Jeremiah, however, that actually correspond to this description of prophetic speech in two essential points. They are the speeches of Jeremiah which were fashioned into a Deuteronomistic type of sermon (a model example: ch. 25:1-14) in which: (*a*) the call to repentance actually stands in the middle, (*b*) the speeches of the prophets were systematized

19

in a manner that is quite similar to the description given by Steuernagel. From this point on, the question — whether this group of speeches belongs to the prophet Jeremiah, or as it is widely assumed today, to a kind of secondary sermon-editing based upon Jeremiah's words — assumes a greater importance.[3]

Finally, it is also important for Steuernagel's description of prophetic speaking that a section on " The Form of the Prophetic Activity " (pp. 463 f.) follows the summary that was just examined. Here we could well expect a description of the prophetic speech forms, for the section previously described leads us almost to the questions: How does an accusation, a warning, or only an announcement of judgment, etc., appear? What form does it have? But this is not asked here. Three major types are only very vaguely mentioned: the larger connected speech, the short precise saying, and the dialogue. This determination of form is just as insufficient and groundless as the citing of prophetic speeches in the previous section was clear and extensive. The reason for this is obvious. It is due to the preconceived idea of the prophet as a speaker who develops a theme. This conception appears forthrightly in one astonishing passage: " Many speeches may have been previously planned, prepared, and then delivered according to this plan. Others are certainly extemporaneous, being called forth by the requirements of the moment. Then they adhered less to a definite theme and the development of this theme in a clear and orderly manner, and the train of thought had a more contingent character."

The particular conception of the prophetic speech present here could hardly be stated more clearly. Consequently, it is understandable that the individual prophetic speech forms do not emerge. This conception would have to collapse if it were shown that the prophets generally have not conceived of speeches in this sense, i.e., having a theme, order of development, train of thought, etc.

It has been shown, therefore, that the conception of the

rhetorical form of prophecy which was found in Baudissin's work was still intact in Steuernagel and determined the whole of his description of the prophetic work. An opposing movement certainly *had* to come, for this view of prophetic speech was too obviously impressed with a modern conception.

The opposing movement could possibly come from two directions: from a critique of this general modernization of prophecy or from a critique of the idea that the prophets could have produced speeches. Both have happened. Hölscher could be cited as an example of the first criticism, and Gunkel an example of the second.

3. G. Hölscher, Die Propheten (*Leipzig, 1914*)

This book stood the prophetic investigation on its head! No greater antithesis can be conceived than between a prophet who composes a speech with a theme, an orderly arrangement, and developed train of thought and a kind of prophetic utterance whose roots lie in the incantation (Hölscher, pp. 89 ff.) :

"The original form of demonic speech is the incantation. It can easily pass over into soothsaying, for the boundaries are fluid. The mantic saying also has magical effects. . . . We find the old soothsaying form in numerous blessings and curses in the old sagas (Gen. 9:25-27; 27:19 f., 28 f.; ch. 49; Deut., ch. 33). A demon originally stood behind the old soothsaying as well as behind all incantations. This distinguishes it from the speeches of later prophecy."

This radical reversal was necessary. At the outset it had to be made clear that the prophet's speaking was so utterly different that it could be clarified not out of the intellectual climate of the nineteenth century A.D., but rather out of its own particular history, prehistory, and the history of the surrounding world.

It can further be acknowledged that the incantation, at

21

least in regard to its genre, stands decidedly nearer to prophetic speech than a well-arranged discourse with a rational conclusion. It is certainly regrettable that these beginnings by Hölscher were not acknowledged to be valuable. The curses and blessings in the Old Testament have still not been subjected to a penetrating investigation and clarification. To be sure, the incantation should not be made into such a leading concept as Hölscher does in the few passages indicated here. An investigation into the broader religio-historical foundation (which would, above all, have to consider the folklore research) might show that the incantation is a distinctive genre, and that the curse and blessing have their own forms as well, and that both, apart from the " mantic saying," might also be recognized as a separate genre in the Old Testament.[4]

Another of Hölscher's observations that is important is that the old soothsaying is to be distinguished from the later prophetic speech in that the " I " of man speaks through it (and, as Hölscher says, the demon speaks through this " I "). Hölscher is only interested, however, in the historical background of the prophetic speech found in the incantation. He generally does not concern himself at all with the speech forms of the prophetic utterances themselves or their history and development. Neither the index nor the table of contents mentions a treatment of the sayings of the prophets or the prophetic speeches. At this point Hölscher, despite all differences with the scholars of his time, stands on the same level as they. First, the prophets themselves interest him as a religio-historical phenomenon, and then the contents of what the prophets said, as an intellectual phenomenon. By raising the question in this manner he did not discover their significance. There is only one thing he has to say concerning this, and that is a thesis which has gradually won general acceptance.[5]

" In even its simplest form the soothsaying has rhythmical form. The Hebrew soothsayer can be compared to the Arabian *kahin;* and the utterance of the *kahin* and of those

22

singers (*shair*) who were related to him was rhythmically formed throughout in the oldest rhythms of Arabian poetry " (pp. 92 f.) .

When this turned out to be correct, the theory of the rhetorical form of prophecy was thereby proved to be erroneous. The exact way in which Steuernagel defended himself against this thesis which was then arising can still be detected in his " Introduction."

" From written versions it appears that the prophetic speeches often tended to have a poetic form. Now and then the prophet may have turned poet, but it is certainly unjustified to maintain as some have done recently that strong poetic rhythms are normal, and to try to shape the prophetic speeches into real verses." [6]

Here a change in the conception of prophetic speech clearly appears before our eyes. The long predominant view of the prophets as preachers or as speakers breaks down. The short rhythmic saying is recognized as the basic unit of prophetic speech. This change is executed in many places with many nuances. In my judgment it is most clearly seen in Gunkel's summarizing essays on prophecy.

4. H. Gunkel, " Propheten II seit Amos," RGG[1]

Gunkel's study begins (A) with the " private experiences of the prophets," the visions, the auditions, and other prophetic experiences with all their accompanying phenomena. Here he resembles Hölscher. Then (B) he shows the outlines of the history of prophecy, but we shall not go into this here. Only then comes (C) " The Literary Work of the Prophets."

It must again be noted here that in this sketch, Gunkel adheres entirely to the old scheme that begins with the question concerning the prophet's experience. Following this he intends to reconstruct the history of prophecy. Only then does he come to the prophets' speeches. These

23

speeches still appear under the title " The Literary Work of the Prophets," and in this as well, Gunkel follows the older descriptions. Later, when the title is properly divided, it becomes evident how tenaciously the old conception could be held that the prophets were the " authors " of their own books.

Gunkel stops short of the complete acceptance of the " ecstatic theory " (essentially stemming from Hölscher), although in the first section he acknowledged that it had some basic significance for prophecy insofar as he accepted the idea that the prophet usually spoke not in but after the ecstasy.

Prophetic speech begins chiefly with short utterances.[7] He finds the oldest level of the prophetic style in the " short, enigmatic words and compound words such as the names which they gave their children (e.g., *Lō' 'ammî*) ." A later phase is that of the short sayings, some two or three lines long (e.g., Isa. 1:2 f.; Amos 1:2; 3:2 f.) . " Then the prophets learned to compose longer speeches. But they consist mostly of a more or less loose agglomeration of sayings, e.g., Isa., ch. 13."

We find here one of the most important results of recent prophetic research which has been accepted by almost all: *The basic unit of prophetic speech is the short saying, the short, single saying which is in itself independent.*

Gunkel establishes two classes of prophetic oracles: visions and auditions. The style of the visions is the narrative; auditions are prophetic speeches that are developed in an almost boundless variety of ways.

This basic division of the prophetic " oracle " into visions and auditions was appropriated without change by Gressmann and developed. In this division of the prophetic speeches into visions and auditions lies the basically erroneous starting point of Gunkel's and Gressmann's genre investigation. It was, nevertheless, frequently appropriated or repeated.

Gunkel says that the visions are in the narrative style, al-

24

though at the outset he separates the narrative (in point 5) from the oracle (which consists of visions plus auditions). The evidence is clear. Next to one another in the prophetic books are accounts (or narratives) and short speeches (later a third major kind will be mentioned). Within the category of accounts is a group of vision accounts. In the prophetic books, however, there is not one single vision account in which the prophet *only* sees. *Always*, without exception, hearing is associated with the experience of seeing. If one wants to use this foreign terminology, it can therefore be said that *all* visions were connected to auditions. That means that *all* vision accounts are at the same time — if one wants to speak in these terms — audition accounts. Both, then, belong to the account as particular forms of the genre. (Even then there are still many other kinds of accounts such as reports of the commissioning which the prophet receives . . .)

Moreover, the prophetic *speeches* (which can also be termed " oracles ") can be clearly distinguished from the accounts. To term all these prophetic accounts as auditions is misleading because this must be understood in analogy to visions. A vision, however, always must be referred to precisely as a vision account. So when one sees the term " audition," he thinks — in analogy to a vision — of an *event* of hearing. Gunkel and Gressmann meant by audition, however, only that which the prophet has heard and now repeats. So a hopeless confusion has originated here. It is time that this false juxtaposing of vision (vision account) and audition (prophetic speech) should be brought to an end.

One will see that the following list also goes beyond that of Steuernagel and is more precise.

" Within the prophetic speeches an almost boundless diversity prevails: promise and threat, a recounting of sins, admonitions, Priestly Torah, historical retrospection, disputations, songs of all kinds, short lyrical passages, liturgies, parables, allegories, etc. . . ."

Here the particulars of this list cannot be discussed. This will have to be done later. Following this, almost at the end of Gunkel's account, is a very astonishing thesis which is most important for the investigation of the genre of the prophetic speech.

" It is basic to the history of this genre that most of those which have been named are not originally prophetic, but are foreign genres which have been extensively appropriated by the prophets. That the prophets have appropriated so extraordinarily many of these is an indication of their passionate contention with the heart of their people. . . .

" Which, then, is the *true* prophetic genre? The oldest prophets are proclaimers of the future. We must, therefore, expect the oldest prophetic style to be found in the passages that depict the future. Some particularly clear examples of this style are the oracles against foreign nations in Isa., chs. 13 to 21; Jer., chs. 46 to 51; and elsewhere. (On the other hand) the new forms used by the prophets would, of course, be found in the passages where they speak to Israel."

The thesis of Gunkel's found in this paragraph placed the investigation of the prophetic speeches on a sidetrack for a long time. The starting point, however, is doubtlessly right and of great significance. The prophets have appropriated a multiplicity of other speech forms so as to deliver their message in forms of speech which are not actually prophetic. More work has been done at this juncture. A great many individual investigations have been made into these foreign speech forms which are found in prophetic speech but were not originally prophetic.[8]

Furthermore, it is clear that another question must now arise: What is the specifically prophetic speech form? If we look back now to the earlier work, we can see that some agreement had been reached on *one* point. The announcement of judgment to their own nation, along with the reason given in the accusation, was recognized by all as the most essential, the most important, or the most frequent prophetic speech form.[9] Gunkel, too, designated it as such along with others. In spite of that he believed the *true* prophetic genre was the oracle against foreign nations. The *one* reason which he gives for this — " the oldest prophets are proclaimers of the future " — turns out to be just as true for the judgment-speech against the prophet's own nation. Only the stylistic characteristics which he collects in points 8–11 remain. It is the element of mystery that he believes is characteristic of the prophetic style: " These revelations in the soul of the prophet have seemed very dark and shadowy and for that reason the characteristic emphasis of these speeches is demonic and enigmatic."

Other characteristics are " the peculiarly limpid style, the extraordinary concreteness, the unusual force of the prophetic passion." It still must be asked, however, whether this is true of only the oracles against the foreign nations or just *especially* of these oracles? This is still a very vague and questionable basis for such a far-reaching thesis. One might also say that the succinct estimation of Isa., chs. 13 to 21, is methodologically very vulnerable. Extraordinarily different kinds of passages, which have the highest probability of stemming from different times, are found together here (it is almost universally agreed that ch. 19 is very late) . In any case no clearly recognizable type of prophetic speech can be seen. It is more significant, however, that this thesis stands in open contradiction to that which was said previously. In point 3, Gunkel had said that the short saying, some two or three lines long, stands at the beginning of the development, and he cited sayings out of Isa., ch. 1, and Amos, ch. 1, as examples. Isaiah, chs. 13 to 21, however, is composed almost altogether of longer units. Only a very few short sayings are found there.

Gunkel's thesis that the oracles against foreign nations are the original or true prophetic speech form stands, therefore, on a very weak footing. It has, accordingly, been accepted by very few others. In spite of that, it has still had a considerable and clearly retarding effect on the further

27

investigation of prophetic speech forms as has been noted above.

One expects in Gunkel's articles a clarification of the relationship of the uniquely prophetic speech genre(s) as he understands them to the others which the prophets only borrowed. One such explanation of this relationship follows, but it is not completely satisfactory.

According to Gunkel, the single prophetic genre was developed in two directions — " The prophets became poets and thinkers." As poets, " the prophets reached deeply into the storehouse of profane and religious lyrics," which must have existed long before them. The individual determination of these borrowed profane and religious genres is exact and comprehensive. Here Gunkel is in his own specialized field of investigation. In the other direction, " the prophets as thinkers," it becomes problematical.

" They have not been satisfied to proclaim the future but began to give a moral reason why this thing must come. . . . Then they attached their threats and ' reproaches ' in which they expose Israel's crimes (Isa. 1:2 f.; Jer. 2:10-13), imitating with predilection the style of a speech before the judge (Isa. 3:13-15; Micah 6:1). For the great judgment prophets, the exposure of sins is an important part of their sermon (Micah 3:8). There are whole prophetic books such as Amos, which exhibit the essentials of both of these genres: the threat (*Drohrede*) and the reproach (*Scheltrede*)."

This passage in Gunkel's essay on the prophetic speech forms is particularly important. Here Gunkel correctly perceives — and is in thorough agreement with previous work (see above) — that the " threat " and the " reproach," which were classed earlier as the accusation or reason and the announcement of judgment (Gunkel can also classify it as such in this section), are actually the major elements of the prophetic proclamation. This must, therefore, be especially underscored because the oracles against foreign nations which Gunkel previously believed to be the most characteristic of prophecy do not contain a *reason* for the judgment that will come upon the people. Gunkel, also, cannot be cited in opposition to the thesis that the major form of the prophetic proclamation is the proclamation of judgment against the prophet's own nation and its grounding in the accusation.

Nevertheless, to place the accusation or the reproach under the title " The Prophets as Thinkers " seems very strange. One cannot very well say that a threat is a way of speaking peculiar to a thinker. What Gunkel meant, however, is clear. The prophets have reflected over why their people may encounter the terrible ill which they must announce. Out of this reflection a reason for the judgment has come to them, " they began to assign a moral reason." That this must occur only in the form of a reproach or " reproaching-speech " is hard to understand, however. When Gunkel then goes on to say that the prophets in this reproaching-speech imitate with predilection the style of speech given before a judge, he departs farther, if possible, from his title, " The Prophets as Thinkers "; but at the same time he comes nearer to the actual form of these prophetic speeches.

If my understanding is correct, the juxtaposing of " threat " and " reproach," which continues to this day, originated in this explanation by Gunkel. With these two terms, however, the lack of clarity in this description was passed on and this has not yet been overcome. When Gunkel placed the " reproach " under the title " The Prophets as Thinkers," and classified it with the speech forms that had been plainly *borrowed,* such as speech forms of the service of worship and of profane songs that were not characteristic of prophecy, it was considered to be one of the speech forms that was borrowed by the prophets. He thus placed it on a different level from the " threat," and therefore from the announcement of judgment. The impression must, therefore, be given that the " threat " and "reproach" represent two independent, originally and natu-

29

rally separate genres which were only secondarily brought into connection with each other by the prophets.

This lack of clarity has produced aftereffects in most of the investigations down to this day. It has caused the evidence that is clear in the texts to remain hidden. This evidence shows that, in actuality, the "threat" and the "reproach" are found in the great majority of the prophetic texts, not as two separate genres, but as *one* speech form, i.e., as two constituent parts or members of *one* speech form — the prophetic judgment-speech.

Moreover, it appears that the two terms in themselves are both open to question. That shall be shown in an excursus. Instead of these terms, I propose to turn back to the terms used previously which were substantially undisputable: the announcement of judgment (or ill) and the reason (or when considered independently, the accusation). I want to emphasize here that it is not the terms as such that concern me (the terms "threat" and "reproach" are not absolutely false) but the lack of clarity which their introduction brought and which today is still with us.

In conclusion it might be pointed out that Gunkel's article on prophecy in the second edition of *RGG* (1930) was reprinted without any essential changes. In his introduction to the volume on the Major Prophets (revised by Hans Schmidt) in the old Göttingen Bibelwerk, 1915, Gunkel gives exactly the same description of the prophetic speeches with the exception that this description is more detailed. Although this introduction to the major prophets appeared after the publication of *RGG*[1], one receives the impression that the description in *RGG* is a summary of this essay. The development is the same and in many places there is a verbatim correspondence. This fact is important insofar as it shows that Gunkel did not find it necessary to change his understanding of prophetic speech as a whole or in part over a long span of time. This is certainly a sign of the originality and far-reaching significance

30

of his understanding; but it is also a sign of the lack of essentially new impulses in this area over a long period of time. This state of things also makes it understandable that the basic definitive lines of the prophetic speech forms drawn by Gunkel were accepted from then on without the necessary corrections being undertaken.

5. H. Gressmann, " Prophetische Gattungen," Der Messias (Göttingen, 1929), Bk. II

This book stands in the period when the prophetic genres were being studied entirely upon the basis that had been worked out by Gunkel. Gressmann's significance lies in the fact that he developed the work farther along the lines which had been laid down by Gunkel and then showed their implications for the history of eschatological speech in the Old Testament. To begin with, it can be quickly perceived wherein Gressmann follows Gunkel.

" The prophets were authors of small prophetic sayings that were intended for oral delivery and have been only secondarily recorded " (p. 69). " The original task of the prophets was to foretell the future, so almost all their sayings are oracles. . . . Beyond that major theme they fall into two groups: the visions or sights, and the auditions or speeches. Under the heading of these, two major genres can be distinguished: the threats and the promises. . . . In the threats one finds the anger of the prophet over the sins of Israel which he reproaches. They are for that reason connected mostly with a reproaching-speech so that the reason may be given for the coming catastrophe."

All of this agrees entirely, and in part exactly, with the lines that Gunkel had laid down. It is to be noted especially that the basic distinction between visions and auditions (i.e., speeches) is simply accepted. On the other hand, he sees more clearly that the distinction between salvation and judgment proclamation is fundamental to the

31

prophetic sayings, and furthermore that " the threats are most of the time connected with a reproach." He has taken over the terms " threatening-speech " and " reproaching-speech " as have most investigators since then.

Gressmann is now particularly interested in the relation of the judgment and salvation announcement, or as he says, threat and promise. Here he sets up and develops a thesis that is decisive for his work and that has had far-reaching effects. He maintains that the oldest form of the oracles accessible to us connects the announcement of salvation and announcement of judgment. And Gressmann, in fact, maintains this in radical antithesis to the literary-critical prophetic investigation that wants to hold that the preexilic prophets could have been *only* judgment prophets, because the salvation sermon must nullify the judgment sermon. Gressmann says, on the contrary, that it might be possible for judgment and salvation to be successive, as in Hosea (p. 71). This was never stated by the prophets, however, but simply presupposed. It must, therefore, have been presupposed as tradition (pp. 71 ff.). This tradition may be witnessed outside of Isarel: " The numerous old Egyptian oracles attest to the formal unity of threat and promise as the original form. . . . Now that we are acquainted with the Egyptian oracle, it is no longer doubtful that the literary-critical school was on the wrong path " (p. 73).[10]

In addition to this religio-historical evidence, Gressmann employs a rather general psychological argument, the thesis of which is not completely trustworthy ("After the rain follows sunshine " [p. 72]. " The prophets along with poets are inspired by changing moods. . . . In times when they are susceptible to more moderate moods they proclaim salvation, at least under certain conditions "). Moreover, this psychological thesis of the changing moods of the prophet contradicts the literary thesis that the basic form of prophetic speech consists of both the salvation- and judgment-speech in one unit. Here it is interesting to note that Gress-

32

mann's thesis of the most original form of prophetic speech coincides with Gunkel's in one passage.

" Salvation and judgment are regularly joined together in the prophecies concerning foreign nations; in any case, it is characteristic of the oldest form of the oracle." (P. 72.)

This assertion concerning the oracle against foreign nations has not proved to be true. It is also not entirely clear how the sentence is meant. Actually it can only mean that in the oracle against foreign nations (e.g., Isa., chs. 34 f.) judgment is announced to the nations, i.e., an enemy nation, and at the same time salvation is proclaimed to Israel. (The other possibility is that in the same speech, first judgment, *and then* salvation is announced to the same foreign nation, e.g., Isa., ch. 19. This occurs too seldom for Gressmann to have meant that here.) There is a similar lack of clarity when reference is made in the same connection to Isa. 28:23-29 and Jer., ch. 1. Certainly both passages show that the prophets have not preached judgment sermons exclusively; but especially the parable in Isa. 28:23-29 expressly states that the judgment and salvation *cannot* occur at the same time.

In the third part (pp. 74–77), Gressmann discusses the preprophetic popular " eschatology " which is presupposed by Amos and against which he polemicized. This discussion is important and is thoroughly substantiated. In the fourth part (pp. 77–86), however, what he proceeds to say concerning the structure and history of salvation and judgment prophecy is only a hypothesis and its basis is very questionable.

" In the beginning threat and promise were a literary unity. With Amos the great alteration begins — the threat which was previously directed against the nations is now directed against Israel. That comes first with Amos. It was so unheard of that it became a special genre. Thus the breach occurred between threat and promise. From this time on each genre had its independent existence and its individual history." (P. 82.)

Just prior to this, Gressmann had shown on the basis of I Kings, ch. 22, that the threat against Israel did not begin with Amos. Another sentence in this section is very noteworthy: " The threatening-speech which was directed against the nations is directed against Israel." Does that not mean that the literary genre remains the same and only changes its addressee? Here he may be partly right. In chs. 1 and 2 Amos used the same speech form in his judgment-speech to the nations as he did in his judgment-speech to Israel. Or, when Isaiah had to announce redemption to his own people in the Syro-Ephraimite War, he did it while giving a judgment-speech against Israel's enemies. Then, however, Gressmann's conclusion — " Thus the breach occurred between threat and promise " (p. 82) — is no longer possible. The presupposition that a combined salvation and judgment announcement stands at the beginning is proved to be a pure hypothesis that is not once adequately substantiated.

In conclusion, Gressmann speaks of structure and style form. An example that shows how little the whole area has been researched is the sentence, " In general the same introductory and concluding formulas are found with the promises." The forms and phrases that Gressmann cites are also chosen rather arbitrarily. Here the statements of Gunkel were much more accurate.

6. J. Lindblom, " Die prophetische Orakelformel," Die literarische Gattung der prophetischen Literatur, Appendix (Uppsala, 1924)

A new period in the research on the prophetic speech forms begins with Lindblom's work.

Beginning with medieval mystical revelation literature which he considers to be a genuine analogy of the prophetic speeches, Lindblom very amply describes the style forms of this revelation account. At many points he accords with Gunkel's description of the prophetic style.

Then in The Book of Amos he indicates what is known as the basic form of prophetic speech — the revelation. The conclusion to which he comes is that The Book of Amos is composed of fifteen of Amos' revelations. In the beginning (chs. 1 and 2) stands the great revelation to the foreign nations in the form of an oracle. Then three follow in the form of sermons: chs. 3:1-11; 4:1-13; 5:1-6. To these are joined three in the form of woes: chs. 5:7-17; 5:18-27; 6:1-7. A revelation in the form of an oath follows: ch. 6:8-14 and three judgment revelations: ch. 7:1-3, 4-6, 7-9. The series of visions is continued in ch. 8:1-3. Between these comes a biographical revelation: ch. 7:10-17. After a sermon revelation, ch. 8:4-14, the collection ends powerfully with the judgment revelation depicting radical annihilation, ch. 9:1-8a. (Then come the additions.)

One senses immediately that the term "revelation," which was not taken from The Book of Amos itself, does not easily include all these different passages and can do so only with the help of explanatory adjectives. When the same form is supposed to include a vision account, judgment speech, biography, and sermon (?), it is obviously too broad and is only an artificial category. Not so much here depends on the results, however, as on the attempt to see them all together from the viewpoint of the speech forms. It was in the appendix that he made a much better approach which is a decisive step in the right direction. It aims at nothing more than investigating a single formula, a single structural element of the prophetic speech: the formula, *kô'āmar yhwh*. This investigation points in the right direction; the specific contrast between the definition of the speech forms of Amos, which fails to view them as a whole from the viewpoint of the forms, and this exact and fruitful investigation of a single formula shows the way in which research must now go.

Only the most important results of this investigation should be spelled out here. Lindblom finds that " the phrase (namely, " thus says Yahweh ") belongs exclusively to prophetic literature and prophetic narratives." This simple discovery is of the utmost importance. It must then be able to tell us something about the nature of prophecy as this is understood in the prophetic books themselves.[10a] It can be concluded from this that " the formula originally may have served to introduce a real oracle." Later it lost this precise meaning; " it is used to introduce every conceivable kind of prophetic statement." At last, " it was generally understood as a self-evident signature of a prophetic statement " (pp. 100 f.). Lindblom pursues the origin of the formula and comes to the conclusion that

" The oracle formula, ' thus says the Lord,' goes back on the one hand to the proclamation formula of old Oriental declarations and decrees, and on the other hand to the formula with which . . . the message was always introduced."

He verifies this conclusion by means of a great number of Oriental parallels which make it evident. He surmises — rightly in my opinion — that the message style is normative in early prophecy, and later, particularly with Ezekiel, the ceremonial proclamation style came more strongly to the forefront.

With this investigation by Lindblom a very significant advance is made in the investigation of individual prophetic speech forms. Parallel to it is L. Köhler's investigation of the messenger's speech, summarized in *Kleine Lichter*, which is fundamental to his work in Deutero-Isaiah. The works of Lindblom and Köhler apparently originated entirely independent of each other though their results show that they made the same discoveries.

7. L. Köhler, " Formen und Stoffe,"
Deuterojesaja, stilkritisch untersucht
(Giessen, 1923) , pp. 102–105; " Der Botenspruch,"
Kleine Lichter *(Zurich, 1945) , pp. 13–17*

Using Isa. 40:1-2, which represents a well-developed variation of the original messenger's speech *(Botenspruch)*,

Köhler elucidates this characteristic form of the prophetic speech. In so doing he works out convincingly and with outstanding clarity the " setting in life " (*Sitz im Leben*) of the profane messenger's speech shown in Bablyonian examples and in Gen. 32:4-6, which has almost the same structure.

" Both examples from Genesis and Exodus show the messenger's speech originating in the order to the messenger as it is recorded in the narrative. The Babylonian examples show its modification along the lines of the letter style. The example from Amos 1:6-8 shows its slight modification along the lines of the prophetic speech. Jeremiah 2:1-2 shows that the order to the messenger can reappear in the prophets as it was in the messenger's speech.

Köhler then investigates the component parts of the messenger's speech in Deutero-Isaiah and comes to the conclusion that " the use of this formula in Deutero-Isaiah is unmistakably freer than in the older prophets." It is accordingly disadvantageous to begin an investigation of the messenger's speech with Deutero-Isaiah. Köhler must limit himself to the investigation of the introductory and concluding formulas without being able to question whether here in Deutero-Isaiah the speech that is introduced as a messenger's speech can *as such,* be characterized in its own forms apart from the introductory formula. In the small outstanding summary in *Kleine Lichter,* Köhler — aside from taking account of the messenger's speech as a whole — goes a step farther. He explains the character of the prophet in Isa. 6:1-10 to be that of a messenger.

" God needs messengers. Isaiah is ready for the office of messenger. The prophets as well as the apostles are messengers. When the prophet prefaces his speech with, ' Thus says the Lord,' it is then a matter of the speech of a messenger which is distinctly separated from, and contrasted with, human speech by this formula. The concept of the messenger's speech gives an important insight into the nature of the actual, historical inspiration of the Bible."

37

In Lindblom's and Köhler's development of the messenger's speech as a prophetic speech form — although this cannot be seen at first — an entirely new direction in the investigation of prophetic speech has been indicated. One can show that best in a comparison of the results of Lindblom and Köhler. Viewed superficially, both have found out the same thing — they have discovered the connection of the prophetic style with the message style. Since Lindblom had the whole of prophecy in view from the first in his discovery, he pursued the possibilities offered by an investigation of the respective formulas for the illumination of the history of prophecy. Köhler, however, has gone a step beyond that. He finds in this message style an important characterization of prophecy as such — the prophets are messengers. As a messenger of God, Isaiah has been called by God into the ministry of a messenger. And he does not overstate the case when he conjectures that " an important insight into the origin of the actual . . . inspiration of the Bible " can be found here.

When he finds the same messenger situation in his examples in Gen., ch. 32; Ex., ch. 4; and Jer. 2:1-2, thus in completely different literary contexts, he has thereby anchored the prophetic speech in a form and to a situation that withdraws it from the arbitrary subjective interpretation derived from various kinds of " prophetic experience." This now forms a tangible, objective starting point for inquiring into the speech of the prophets. A comparison with Lindblom shows just that. We have pointed out above the striking contrast between Lindblom's investigation of individual speech forms and his far too general and vague collective categorization of the Amos speeches under the concept of " revelation." Now we can see the reason for that. Lindblom has *not* drawn the conclusion that the speeches of Amos are *messenger's* speeches and have thus received their structure from the message form. For Lindblom this new starting point is hidden behind the concept of revelation which is obtained from some place *other* than

38

the message situation. Now it can be seen even more clearly that the speeches of Amos as such, are *certainly not* revelations. They are not *revelations* in the sense of something which was revealed to Amos, but are words of a messenger; and that is an essential distinction. We will see later that this distinction has been seen and elucidated especially by R. B. Y. Scott. It can already be clearly seen in reading Lindblom's works. There isn't any connection between his investigation of the messenger formula and the religio-historical examples — the revelations of the mystics — with which he began. It is evident that this analogy is only very partial, for one cannot say that the mystics were messengers and understood themselves as messengers in the same way that this can be said of the prophets. Now, from this point we come back once more to Köhler. So long as one traced the *speeches* of the prophet back primarily to their " private experiences " (Gunkel), the subjective factor of the expositors in this interpretation was simply too strong because the prophets themselves say so little about these experiences. Most of this had to be inferred, thus leaving too much room for the imagination or understanding of the interpreter.[11] If one can begin the inquiry about the speeches of the prophets with the basic knowledge that they are messengers who bring a message and speak in the style of a message, then there is a foundation of formulas, speech forms, and speeches which have been passed down, where one can be assured of encountering the self-understanding of the prophets and of being on solid ground. Of course this does not answer all our questions, nor does it place a miraculous key into our hands. What has been found here is nothing more than a methodological starting point; but this basis should now be confidently accepted. This has happened, e.g., in the work of Wildberger and H. W. Wolff (see below). The question that was posed by Köhler has already been outlined above: Is the characterization of the prophetic word as a messenger's speech to be limited to its *framework,* i.e., to the introductory and concluding for-

39

mulas, or can the body of the prophetic speeches be understood as a messenger's speech? Posing the question in another way: When regarding prophetic speech as a messenger's speech, can one so separate form and content that he can say that only the form (i.e., framework) is related to a messenger's speech and that the content is arbitrarily different, entirely independent of the introduction and conclusion? Lindblom has already shed light in a very important way upon this question in his discovery that in the beginning the formula " thus says Yahweh " was the introduction of *only* the oracle, but later came to be the formal way of designating every prophetic speech. It is already clear from this whether or not the *content* of the messenger's speech can be also determined by the messenger's situation.

8. *E. Balla,* Die Droh- und Scheltworte des Amos (*Leipziger Reformationsprogramm, 1926*)

This thorough and very carefully executed investigation of the speech forms of Amos shows, first, that the work on the speeches of the prophets still continues on the course laid out by Gunkel. The description of the style of the threat sounds extraordinarily similar to what Gunkel said about this in his article in *RGG*. One sees that the major terms " threat " and " reproach " have become so common that they are no longer substantiated. Besides this, one can see a close proximity to Gunkel's understanding of the prophets, especially with regard to the origin of the speeches in their " private experiences." How little the suggestions of Lindblom and Köhler were heard at this time is seen in the investigation of the introductory and concluding formulas where their relation to the messenger situation is not mentioned. They are only termed " proclamations," " imperatives," and " conclusion."

In spite of that, this work shows that the problem of the

investigation of prophetic speech forms is recognized as essential to the understanding of the prophets and it is regrettable that it has found so few followers. The work contains a great number of important observations, but only a few can be mentioned here. At the outset Balla delineates the units. He distinguishes between a pure threat — a threat with a reason (i.e., reproach) — and a pure reproach (only in Amos 5:12 and 6:12). The result of this is that the units which are ascertained by him are, *almost without exception,* threats with a reason. The theoretical postulation that the two most important forms of prophetic speech are the reproach and the threat is not confirmed by the text. The textual units almost without exception contain combinations, e.g., " the threat with a reason." Here we come extremely close to the consequence that the true prophetic unit is the judgment-speech composed of an announcement of judgment with a reason; but the traditional way of speaking of the threat and the reproach as equal independent units is already too deeply entrenched.

Now Balla has made a very important observation concerning the history of the prophetic speech. He has gone into the history prior to the Major Prophets in order to compare the speeches of Amos with the earlier speeches that were passed down in the historical books.

" Originally the genre probably existed only in the form of a pure threat with a brief reason. The utterance was a recounting of a vision or audition. With Amos the strong connection with this mysterious inner experience is already broken. Even if most of the time he still reports only what Yahweh has allowed him to see or what Yahweh has said to him, he, nevertheless, still threatened and reproached himself occasionally, and when doing so, he was certain of his conviction that he was speaking completely in accord with Yahweh. . . .

" Along with this a still further development of the genre is seen in the reproaches that Amos himself delivers. Originally the accent lay fully on the threat. It is still there in

41

most of the cases with Amos. In the reproaches that he delivers himself, a shifting of accent almost imperceptibly takes place (esp. ch. 6:1-7). The exposure of sins starts to become a more important part of the prophetic task (compare Matt. 23:13-33, which is the final stage of this development)."

This observation presupposes that indeed both parts of the prophetic judgment-speech originally formed a unit. It has now been very clearly perceived that the announcement was originally the predominant part of this whole, and was the *real* word of God with only a very limited reason. In giving the *reason* the prophet himself gradually comes more into the forefront, thereby changing the character of the prophetic speech. This is remotely related to Lindblom's observation that the messenger formula originally introduced only true oracle but gradually became a formalized introduction to all prophetic speeches. That is to be joined to Balla's observation that in many cases with Amos only the announcement (the threat) is explicitly designated as Yahweh's word rather than the *whole* prophetic speech. The significance of this observation can only be shown later in another context.

There is still another observation of Balla's that is important and leads us in the right direction. In his treatment of the judgment-oracle (part 12) he begins with an early form that he finds in I Kings 22:17 (Micaiah ben Imla) and otherwise in Isa. 21:1-10; Jer. 46:2-6. It is clear that here Gunkel's thesis that the earliest form of prophetic oracle is the oracle against foreign nations has been adopted. The characteristics that Balla presents as being common to all three passages correspond exactly to Gunkel's characterization of this early form of the oracle. With the examples selected by Balla, it becomes clearer than Gunkel had made it that an agreement in essential stylistic elements can be found here. The early passage in I Kings 22:17 is particularly important in this regard. It reads (in the translation of Balla):

42

He (Micaiah) said:
  I saw all Israel scattered " on " the mountains
  as sheep, which have no shepherd
And Yahweh said:
  They have no master!
  Each one may return in peace to his home!

It is certainly not accidental that Balla does not offer a comparable " judgment-oracle " from Amos, for there is no speech by Amos that corresponds to it. But even more there is an utterly striking distinction between the kind of judgment-oracle such as I Kings 22:17 (further developed in Isa. 21:1-10 and Jer. 46:2-6) and the announcement of judgment in the eighth-century prophets. Balla has also sensed that, and because of this, he speaks — and rightly so — of a later mixing of styles which may be recognized in Isa. 5:11-13 and 17:12-14. In the first case Balla explains, " The style of the oracle has penetrated the genre of the reproach and threat "; in the second case, " The style of the threat has influenced the style of the oracle." This means, therefore, that Balla sees that we are actually dealing with two genres having different roots which have first become related through the mixing of styles: the judgment-oracle (type 1, I Kings 22:17) and the " threat." [12]

The perfectly clear distinction here is that the " judgment-oracle " is given directly as the vision of a seer (I Kings 22:17), while the announcement of judgment is something essentially different, namely, a messenger's speech introduced by the messenger formula. The conclusion that is unavoidable here is that we are dealing with two speech forms that are different in regard to their roots: *the seer's oracle (Seherspruch) and the messenger's speech.* Balla is right in showing that mixed forms of both genres can already be recognized in the prophecy of the eighth century. We can, on the other hand, ascertain a special independent form of the seer's oracles (in Num., chs. 22 to 24), which from the viewpoint of its origin has *nothing* to do with the prophetic speech (the messenger's speech). But before the writing prophets, the seer's oracle and the messenger's speech must have already been related with one another as I Kings, ch. 22, shows. This would correspond to the development of the office of seer into that of the prophet.[18]

It seems to me that the work of Balla already comes close to this conclusion. More attention must then be given to the relationship of the seer's oracle to the prophetic speech.

A further investigation of the speech forms of the individual prophets can best be considered after the work of Balla even if it was done considerably later.

9. R. B. Y. Scott, " The Literary Structure of Isaiah's Oracles," Studies in Old Testament Prophecy (Edinburgh, 1950), pp. 175–186

Scott distinguishes between five major kinds of speeches:

1. Autobiographical narratives, which include oracles (chs. 6:1-13; 8:1-8, 11-18).

2. Private oracles connected to the public oracles, usually as their introduction (chs. 5:9; 22:14, 15; 30:8).

3. Public oracles (ch. 1:2-3, 4-9, 10-17, etc.).

4. Biographical narratives of a primary kind (ch. 7:1-17).

5. Biographical narratives of a secondary kind (chs. 36 to 39).

The oracle as such has four basic forms: threat, reproach, promise, and exhortation. The first two forms are the most frequent and are often found joined together. The promises, for the most part, are later insertions.

The major forms in Isaiah that are outlined above completely correspond to the works of Gunkel discussed previously. It is not necessary to go into the particulars of that here. Chapters 1, 4, and 5 correspond to both groups, which Wildberger (perhaps more practically) terms a third-person account (*Fremdbericht*) and personal account (*Eigen-*

44

bericht). For private and public oracles one could say more simply — speeches to the people and speeches to the individual. With these slight changes one can concur with Scott's classification. But a difficulty arises with the more exact definition of " oracle." Here there are two questions to be raised: (1) Is the exhortation to be placed alongside the other three as a basic prophetic genre? There is in any case the other possibility that where the exhortation appears entirely independent (as in ch. 1:10-17), it is a " borrowed " genre, namely " prophetic Torah." Where single exhorting sentences are found, we are possibly dealing with an expansion that does not represent an independent genre. (2) Threat and reproach are treated as originally independent genres in the manner of Gunkel and Gressmann (even if it is added that frequently they are found joined together). The same thing is true here that was said regarding Balla's work. From his own point of view, Scott would certainly have represented the unity of the two as being primary if he had not followed the traditional division.

What Scott says concerning the specific prophetic formulas, on the basis of this introductory definition of speech forms, does not go beyond what has already been achieved, i.e., Scott (similar to Balla) does not see the value which these formulas have for the characterization of the prophetic speech as a messenger's speech.

Following this introduction, Scott deals with the four forms that, according to him, are basic to all oracles. First of all is the reproach (pp. 179–181). Here an observation can be made about Scott's work which enables one to see in an impressive way how the text itself again and again prevails over expositions that are on the wrong path. In his investigation of the structure of the reproach, Scott comes to the following conclusion:

" The core of the reproach is a literally described complaint, usually with one principal point and embodied in a single verse (ch. 5:20, 21; 7:13). . . . . In chs. 8:11-12; 10:1-22; 28:7-8 this is expanded by a statement of the further consequences of the behavior condemned."

In these words the structure of this part of the prophetic judgment-speech is correctly described. As a matter of fact, it is defined not as a " reproach " but as a complaint. And in this way a structure is recognized again that contains this complaint: It consists of a short complaint that is composed primarily of one sentence which most often follows a development. This development shows in some way the consequences of the guilt that was designated in the preceding short sentence. I have come to the same definition of this part of the prophetic speech independently of Scott and presume that it has been perceived in the individual exposition of many exegetes. Examples may be produced in abundance for this structure; and certainly these are to be found not only in Isaiah but in all preexilic judgment prophets.

Now under point 2 we find the threat. Here Scott's investigation of this form in Isaiah touches on Balla's corresponding study of Amos. Scott, also, comes very close to the recognition that both parts form a unity: " Not seldom a reproach appears in a subordinate clause as the ground for the judgement " (a long series of passages follows). It is significant that Scott, in this observation, leaves the designation " threat," whose meaning is basically foreign, and speaks of " judgment." In regard to the texts, the understanding that naturally emerges from them is that they are concerned with an announcement of judgment.

In correspondence with the preceding section, Scott finds a two-membered structure also in the announcement of judgment. He says that frequently doom is literally described and then illustrated in pictorial concepts. In my opinion, one can find a still more exact definition of both members of the announcement of judgment (see below). It is of primary importance that here Scott has seen that both parts of the announcement of judgment are again subdivided in themselves.

The third form, the promise, cannot be explored farther

here. I would like to note in regard to this that the statements are very vague and that the structure of the salvation-speech (or of more types) has not yet been found.

What Scott says in particular about the exhortation (4) only serves to underscore the question raised above of whether we are dealing in general here with an independent form. This investigation of an individual prophet shows, namely, that the exhortation is encountered in connection either with the promise (chs. 7:4-6; 10:24), with the threat (ch. 7:12-13), or with the reproach (ch. 1:16-17). Outside of these Scott must admit that a common structure cannot be found. It is thus a misunderstanding to classify it alongside the basic forms as being of equal importance.

At the conclusion of his investigation (p. 185) is found a very noteworthy comment concerning the relation between the public oracle (we would say the "messenger's speech") and the original speech that the prophet received.

"There are indications that the power of the word (Isa. 8:10; Jer. 20:9) became articulated in their minds as a brief enigmatic sentence or phrase, or even as a single word (Amos 8:1-3; Jer. 1:11-16)." (Such a word required development and clarification.) "These are embryonic oracles and become the texts of oracles for public utterance." Examples are Isa. 8:3-4; 30:8-9; the names in chs. 7:3, 14; 8:3. In ch. 5:7 the word play suggests a primary oracle. Scott cites another large number of different passages as possible indications of this. They all contain the quintessence of a longer oracle.

"It seems probable that they preserve the prophet's first articulations of the 'Word' which JHWH was putting into his mind and on his lips."

In saying this, Scott again adopts a thesis of Gunkel's. But that which still gave the strong impression of being a purely psychological attempt at explanation with Gunkel is with Scott more strongly based on the text. He distinguishes between primary (or embryonic — the designation

47

is helpful) and developed oracles. These, however, already contain elaboration, clarification, and reflection. They are reflections of the word of God which was received originally, but they do not represent it with photographic accuracy. We will come across the same question in the work of Wolff and Wildberger.

10. *H. Wildberger,* Jahwewort und prophetische Rede bei Jeremia (*Zurich, 1942*)

Wildberger asks: " Is the whole tradition of the prophetic books identical with the word of Yahweh, or have the prophets spoken their own word in addition to this? In what relation does each stand to the other? " (P. 4.)

The work of Wildberger is important as an attempt to raise the question from the viewpoint of the prophetic speech forms, as to the relation of the word of God and the word of the prophet in the prophetic book which has been passed down to us. It needs to be completed by a third factor, however, that being the third voice in The Book of Jeremiah — the voice of tradition. To be sure, Wildberger comes to the conclusion that " the prophet is not only a proclaimer but at the same time an interpreter (*Hermeneut*) of God's word." But the criteria used to distinguish God's word from man's word — the formula used in proclamation, the style form, and the literary genres — remain uncertain. The emphasis of the work lies on the investigation of the proclamation formula. Here Wildberger begins with Köhler's definition of the prophetic speech as a messenger's speech (Lindblom is named in the bibliography, but it is not clearly stated that he made the same findings independently of Köhler) and categorizes the proclamation formulas according to their function in the messenger's speech.

It is not possible to distinguish between the true words of Yahweh and the prophet's words simply on the basis of

48

the fact that they are introduced by the messenger formula. Rather, according to Wildberger, the evidence shows that the messenger formula is found in 67 of the 107 genuine speeches of Yahweh and is missing in 40 of these speeches. It is found before 67 genuine words of Yahweh and 14 that are not genuine. In 26 places it is used incorrectly. This is by no means an unambiguous situation, but rather, quite a confused one.

The second criterion is the style. Wildberger must concede even here that " the style also is not always a useful means of separating the word of Yahweh even if it is far more reliable than the formulas " (p. 74) .

The third criterion is the literary genre. Here Wildberger adopts without change the classification of Eissfeldt (*Einleitung,* pp. 88–93) , who does not understand prophetic speech as a messenger's speech as does Köhler, and Wildberger following him. Wildberger must inevitably encounter a conflict with this classification because here two basically different conceptions of prophetic speech meet. Corresponding to this the criterion of the genre plays the same as no role at all in Wildberger's conclusions.

The valuable investigation of the introductory formulas contains a great number of indicative points, however, which are important for defining the speech forms in The Book of Jeremiah more precisely. But always the presupposition for such a definition is the consideration of the third factor — the gradual formation of The Book of Jeremiah by the tradition, i.e., by those who passed it down. Here it seems to me that Wildberger does not look at The Book of Jeremiah deeply enough, especially in respect to the text. The important work of Mowinckel, *Zur Komposition des Jeremiabuches* (1914) , is not named in his bibliography and Rudolph's commentary (1942) was not yet available to him. Order and meaning come into the quite confused situation regarding the usage of the formulas if one once presupposes, as a working hypothesis, the thesis that there were three strata in The Book of Jeremiah. Mowinckel proposed this thesis and it was later adopted by Rudolph. One can see that there is a history that extends from the collection of the authentic words of Jeremiah (Mowinckel's strata A) to the Baruch narrative (B) to the Deuteronomic level (C). Formula g, " The word that came to Jeremiah from Yahweh," which Wildberger seeks to prove as inauthentic, belongs only to the C-strata. The same is also true for the formula " Thus said Yahweh to me." Everywhere the introduction of the third-person account (Formula II) belongs clearly to the Baruch narrative (so too with Wildberger, p. 33).

The difficulty stemming from such extremely different kinds of usages of the messenger formula is clarified, at least in part, by its different usages in the three strata.

In regard to the messenger formula, Wildberger makes an important observation on p. 48. He distinguishes it from the introductory formula, " The expressions ' introductory ' and ' proclamation formula,' taken strictly, are appropriate only for Formulas I, II, and III; . . . the formula $k\hat{o}$ '$\bar{a}mar$ $yhwh$, however, is itself already component of the word of Yahweh."

This observation could easily have been substantiated and extended by showing that the messenger formula is found in the earliest prophetic speeches that have been passed down to us, while many introductory formulas occur first in Jeremiah. But since Wildberger limits himself only to the usage of the formulas in Jeremiah and does not take their prior history into consideration at all, he could not discover the true function and the place of origin of the messenger formula. He says on p. 53: " We must presume that it (the messenger formula) is at the head of each word of Yahweh which is declared by the prophet to the public." But that does not correspond at all to the actual situation as shown by the statistics that were cited above. Wildberger gives a clarification of that on p.74 in noting that the individual speech of Yahweh is often connected with the speech of the prophet through $l\bar{a}k\bar{e}n$ or $k\hat{i}$. Approaching the matter

50

from the other side, he sees the same situation (pp. 113 ff.) in that through the " causal relation " the speech of the prophet provides the reason for the speech of Yahweh. All of that appears very complicated. In actuality it is the very simple situation that has already been encountered in different investigations but always explained differently; namely, the messenger formula has its proper place not as an introduction to the prophetic speech, but as a connective between the reason and the announcement of judgment.

The reason has no introduction whatever in the early prophetic speech. The messenger formula moves quite gradually from its original place to the beginning of the *whole* speech. This is the first effect of the tendency (seen correctly by Wildberger) to designate not only the proclamation but the *whole* prophetic speech as the word of God.

After dealing with all the formulas, Wildberger says (pp. 48 ff.) : " A complete account of a revelation that has come to the prophet is composed of the following elements:
" a) Revelation formula (Formulas I and II)
" b) Prophetic commission
" c) Summons
" d) Messenger formula
" e) Messenger-speech
" f) Middle or concluding formula."

The complete form of this revelation account may be ascertained, but any number of parts can be missing from it. The bare messenger-speech — " thus the word Yahweh " — might also be understood as a revelation account reduced to the minimum.

Here Wildberger gives the impression that the tradition of The Book of Jeremiah might consist of only " revelation accounts." It must be said in answer to this that The Book of Jeremiah contains at least *two* forms of tradition: the account of the utterance of a prophetic speech (as a personal or third-person account) and the plain word of the prophet. Both of these traditional forms may be followed through the whole of the prophetic literature. In addition

51

to this there is a third form. While the prophetic utterance deals with a word that came forth from God and was directed through the prophets to men, there is as well the utterance that is directed from men to God. In Wildberger's second part, "The Prophetic Speeches," this is not distinguished; e.g., the laments of Jeremiah (but also those of the people) are grouped with the prophetic speeches of Jeremiah. He describes the relation of them and the prophetic speech to the word of Yahweh as being causal, explicative, and adversative. This hides the fact that the laments of Jeremiah involve an essentially different kind of speech. One must leave the question of genuineness completely aside at first and pay attention to the evidence that has been passed down to us.

There are also words of lament, plea, and praise to be considered in the prophetic books. This provides a basic classification for defining the forms of prophetic speech which starts with the prophetic books as they were passed down to us. It undertakes the division from the perspective of this very wide circle, lifts the prophetic speeches out of their setting, and *only then* attempts to divide and to define them more closely. The advantage of this procedure is that we can begin with *all* of the prophetic books at the common end-stage of the tradition process — with the whole body of material that is designated by the final stage of the tradition as prophecy or prophetic tradition. From this quite secure basis the inquiry can then be moved back step by step in the direction of the words of the prophets, to the specific prophetic speech forms, and finally to the prophets as the messengers of God bearing the word of God.

11. J. Hempel, " Der Prophetenspruch," Die althebräische Literatur und ihr hellenistisch-jüdisches Nachleben *(Potsdam, 1934) , pp. 56–68*

Hempel's description of prophetic speech corresponds somewhat to Gunkel's work. It will be of particular interest to us here, however, to see the extent to which the whole view of prophetic speech in Hempel's survey has changed from that of Gunkel.

Hempel begins by employing a general definition of prophetic speech as the word of God. This rests upon the fact that prophetic speech, delivered in the first person as the word of God, predominates throughout the whole history of prophecy. From the viewpoint of this general consideration Hempel clarifies the " announcement formula," " Thus says the Lord." To the word of God, in the strict sense, the prophet himself can add various comments concerning the divine " I," the addressee of the message (at this point Hempel sees an approximation of the messenger's speech and herald's call) , and the particular situation. These originated in connection with the writing of the speech. The expansions can be seen especially in the reason. By degrees prophetic speech grew into an expression of personal thought and independent reflections, and therefore, came to approach the sermon. One sees the earliest stage of the origin of the word of God in the oracles that include the reason in the word of Yahweh. Here prophetic speech comes very close to ecstasy, i.e., the ecstatic motion creates the spiritual disposition (see also Hölscher) , but the meaning of the experiences must develop out of faith in God which was already in the soul of the prophet before this. In addition to that, there is the rational elaboration — the ecstatic experience must be translated into rational speech. The nearer we are to the prophetic word as it was originally received, the less reflection it contains, and the more strongly the ecstatic complex of sounds, which was its original core, is able to shine through.

The path of prophetic speech leads from the terse ecstatic oracle uttered in the form of the divine " I " to larger units in the following way: (a) in primary rationalization in which reasons develop, (b) in secondary elaboration in which warning, exhortation, and the cry of woe are added as expressions of the personal involvement of the prophet. The more the obligatory form of the ecstatic experience

53

gave way, the more freedom the prophet acquired for such subjective additions; also, the stronger the influence of foreign style forms became, the more extensive the composition. But the origin of the more developed genres already takes place *before* Amos. Amos is not the beginning, but a point of culmination.

Finally, Hempel gives the following division of the prophetic speech. On the whole, he differentiates between " predicative speeches " and " epic genres." These include descriptions of the time of salvation, of judgment, and of visions. The predicative speeches are divided thus:

unconditional: Threatening-speech
               Salvation-speech
               Reproaching-speech
conditional: Exhortation
               Repentance-speech
               Conditional promise

In Scott's work, as we have seen, his five groups fall into two large groups: accounts and speeches. Hempel's " epic genres " is equivalent to the first group and " predicative speeches " to the second. Behind his division of these into " conditional " and " unconditional " stands the correct understanding of the distinction between primary and secondary (borrowed) prophetic speech forms — similar to what Gunkel had seen. In contrast to Scott, Hempel was certainly correct in seeing that the exhortation (along with the repentance-speech and conditional promise) belongs to the secondary forms. (See Scott above.) An important objection is to be raised, however, against the simple classification of the threat, the salvation-speech, and the reproach together. A judgment-speech would still have to correspond to the salvation-speech and this correspondence would only be seen when the judgment-speech is recognized to be a unit consisting of the threat and the reproach. In another place (p. 61), however, Hempel says it somewhat differently. Here he sees the original form of the pro-

54

phetic speech " in the oracles which include the reason within the word of Yahweh." That means that Hempel sees the original form in the *unity* of the judgment-speech containing the announcement of judgment and its (limited) reason.

None of the work of the previously mentioned investigators clearly proved that the threat and reproach first existed independently and then were sometimes combined secondarily with the prophetic speech. On the contrary, in *all* of the works one can recognize that the more exact investigation of the text leads directly to reckoning with the prophetic word as a unit having two sections that belong together — the accusation and its reason. In Hempel (and similarly in Balla and Scott) it is *clearly* evident that both parts are not to be simply termed alike, but that the " threat " is the real word of God and the " reproach " is in a way more the word of the prophet. While following the history of the research one can quite clearly observe how an essential understanding of the form of the prophetic speech gradually emerges into view more clearly. It was assumed very early (actually by Baudissin) that the actual, original prophetic speech must be short. Now one must gradually grope slowly forward toward the more exact definition of this quite short original oracle. Gunkel ascertained, and in fact, firmly established this conclusion as such (that the original prophetic utterance is quite short) , but he went astray in wanting to find this short form primarily in the oracles against the foreign nations. Hölscher bases the same understanding upon other considerations, but remains so much within the psychological field he scarcely questions the text itself.

In the work of Balla, Scott, Hempel, and others it gradually becomes clear that the *true* prophetic speech is to be found more easily and directly in the announcement than in its reason. This cannot become clear because Gunkel's classification of the " reproach " and " threat " as *independent* units caused their actual relationship to each other as

55

members of *one* speech to remain unclear. Nevertheless, it cannot be justly maintained that both should be independent, for it is very clear that there is a quite definite, recognizable way to relate the one to the other. This relationship is so obvious that in every case it is defined in the same way — as a reason related to its object or as an announcement that is supported by an accusation. At this point, however — there was only one more short step to this clarification — the division of *all* prophetic speeches suddenly changes. In the place of an indefinite number of single forms (compare, e.g., Hempel's list), the simple categorization of the announcement of judgment (" reproach " and " threat ") and of the announcement of salvation as independent units had to come. Then *all* other forms such as exhortation, warning, prophetic Torah, complaint, song, etc., fell quite automatically into a subservient relationship to both of the basic forms — judgment- and salvation-speeches. Basically Gunkel had almost said that already when he contrasted the " borrowed " forms of the prophets', to the genuine prophetic forms of speech.

This understanding of the prophetic speech form is supported in a significant way by a completely different, much stronger theologically defined view of prophecy.

12. H. W. Wolff, " Die Begründung der prophetischen Heils- und Unheilssprüche," ZAW, *1934, pp. 1 ff.* Das Zitat im Prophetenspruch (*Munich, 1937*)

This work in *ZAW* by Wolff in 1934 is, so far as I can tell, the first attempt to make an extensive investigation of prophetic speech forms. It goes into the relation of the single parts of the prophetic speech to one another and encompasses the breadth of the whole of prophecy. Soon one can see that the limits of this horizon have been extended too far in both directions; there are many elements of prophetic speech that cannot be so easily grouped into a few

56

patterns (p. 1, " four types into which nearly all the speeches can be grouped "). Prophecy in the eighth century does not speak the same language as that of the seventh and not at all that of the sixth. Above all, however, the relationship of the " speech about the future [*Zukunftswort*]," and the reason cannot be defined in the salvation-speech as it was in the judgment-speech. If one sees this limit of the investigation, which is understandable in a work that was the first to penetrate an area that had scarcely been touched, then it appears all the more clearly that these results are valuable and go decisively beyond the previous works.

The most important new theme is already indicated in the title. The previously so-called " reproach," which is now designated as the " reason," is no longer to be treated as an independent prophetic speech form but as a part of a unified whole. To be sure, that happens without disputing the view that was generally predominant at the time, and perhaps also without consciously representing a basically different view of prophetic speech. But the fact remains that it is understood here as a whole consisting of a " speech about the future " and a reason. The different ways in which the speech about the future and the reason are related need not be considered here. The important thing is only that Wolff finds a " standard form " among the different possibilities of such a relationship. " The reason, as a declaratory sentence, is joined to the threat with *lākēn, 'al kēn*, or similar connectives." Wolff designates this as the regular form because of its frequent appearance, and also because it makes possible the clarification of other structures (p. 2). It seems to me that here a basic form of prophetic speech has been seen and correctly defined.

Then comes the second observation, which almost had to result from the first; the preparation for it had been made, or it had already more or less been seen in the foregoing works. (See above.)

" In some speeches the prophet's speech and the threatening word of God are clearly separated. . . . The threat is *that* part of the speech *which the prophet has received* and repeats (as the messenger formula shows) . . . . On the other hand, the reason appears as a piece of prophetic reflection and thus lies in a different (later) sphere from that of the revealed word. . . . That the reason was frequently placed first shows that the facts which the reason was based upon preceded the decision of God to send judgment." (Pp. 6 f.)

" Through the reason, the prophet developed from a mere messenger into a mediator. When he gives instructions about the future he announces what is coming and when he gives a reason with it he formulates it himself." [14] (P. 21.)

The fundamental definition of the basic form of prophetic speech is given in these two observations: (*a*) the " regular form " of prophetic speech is a unity consisting of the reason and the announcement, (*b*) the real messenger's speech (i.e., word of God) is the announcement. No one has refuted it since this work by Wolff, but unfortunately it has been adopted only infrequently and developed very little. In my opinion, further work upon the prophetic speech forms must begin with these two observations.

The investigation of prophetic speech forms in H. W. Wolff's work *Das Zitat im Prophetenspruch* (1937) is limited to a typical speech form, the citation, and specifically the citation of human words (the word of Yahweh in the form of a messenger's speech could also be understood as a citation) . In regard to the question being pursued here, this work by Wolff both confirms and adds support to the results that emerged from the earlier investigation. Beyond that, however, it contains a development that cannot be easily recognized and perhaps needs to be made more precise for its meaning to appear clearly.

1. Wolff states here more consciously and emphatically that he can go no farther along the beaten path with many previous investigators who sought to understand and to de-

58

fine prophecy from the viewpoint of prophetic experience.

In the foreword he says, " It is all the less understandable to me why Old Testament research has expended so much effort on an explanation of prophetic psychology in order to come closer to the ' essence ' of prophecy *instead of holding true to the given word* " (p. 3) . There is a sentence corresponding to this at the beginning of the summary: " We do not have a more direct way to the prophet than through his own word. . . . The prophet is the man who is wholly grasped by revelation. This claim separates the prophet from the mystic as well as the ecstatic and one who gives oracles " (pp. 89–91) .

These sentences make it clear that in the study of the history of forms, there is no question of an alien method being imposed upon the text. It is, rather, one that is simply concerned with allowing the text itself to speak without prejudice.

It is presupposed in this investigation that the prophets are messengers and their speeches are messenger's speeches; here Wolff follows Köhler and Lindblom:

" The essence of prophetic speech is . . . the transmission of the word of Yahweh. The presupposition of this is thus that revelation occurs through clear speech." (P. 9.) " In the style of the messenger-speech, the ' I ' of God is the proper subject of the speech." (P. 10.)

The investigation of the citation in the prophetic speech, i.e., of the words of other men which are cited by the prophets, confirms both results of the previous work, namely, that the prophetic speech forms a unity consisting of an announcement and its reason:

" Yahweh's word and deed are not arbitrary. At the outset a reason for the coming judgment is indicated by the prefatory disclosure of guilt which also takes place in the citation." (P. 73.) " The citation is necessary because an altercation is demanded by the dispute between God and man. The speech that only gives an imperative about the future and does not contain an altercation with the hearer

59

is thus actually unprophetic." (P. 92.)

" The salvation- and judgment-speech is set off as a speech that has been received from Yahweh, by the formula, *kô 'āmar yhwh,* and others related to it, whereas the reason, being the prophet's own words, stands completely outside of this framework." (P. 71.)

This is grounded upon a detailed investigation of the citations which shows that they are, by and large, constructions of the prophet himself.

" The citation is subject to the freedom of the prophetic proclamation. It is an instrument of his public speech." (P. 50.) " Because of this it is impossible to make a strict distinction between authentic and inauthentic (i.e., composed by the prophet) citations. The citation does not belong to the realm of the ' private experiences.' Either the prophet has heard it in the street like other people, or . . . he has formulated the citation on the basis of his knowledge of the heart of the people." (P. 72.)

Beyond that the origin of the style of part of these citations can be recognized in the judicial life, in the lawsuit procedure:

" The citation is necessary because the dispute between God and man demands an altercation." (P. 92.) " The sinfulness of man's word before God is exposed by the citation." (P. 93.) " The speeches have the sharpness and unambiguity of the accuser, and at the same time the circumspection of the judge. One of the origins of the citation is the judicial life." (P. 62.) " The usage of the citation first originated in spontaneous speech before men, not in the reception of a revelation; *the prophet* accuses men." (P. 26.) " The lawsuit procedure is the stylistic background of the prophetic citation." (P. 69.) " With the citation, it is as though the prophet allows the accused to accuse themselves."

This was quoted so extensively in order to make it clear that here the " reproach," as an independent prophetic speech form, is completely dropped. In the context of the

60

whole prophetic speech it serves as the reason, but when this part is considered independently it is an accusation.

2. Up to this point, nothing essentially new is contained in these citations beyond the two results which were produced by the earlier work; these were only established more securely and defined more exactly. This work does give further insight, however, into the structure of the prophetic speech. Within the prophetic speech, the citation has a fixed place which can be defined as follows:

" The regular place in the prophetic speech where the citation frequently recurs is in the reason for the judgment. It is the clearest form of the reason." (P. 73.)

If that is correct, then the understanding of the structure of the prophetic speech can go beyond the determination of the two parts, announcement and reason. The second sentence just cited needs to be revised only a little in order to carry Wolff's results a step farther: The citation that exposes " the sinfulness of man's word before God " (p. 93) is *one part* of the reason, but not a kind of reason. The reason itself has two parts, and this bifurcation is usually easy to recognize although it is never schematic. The usual form has the accusation at the outset in a single, usually short sentence. Following that comes a development of the accusation which can be quite varied; very often, however, the words of the accused are adduced in a citation. Wolff's statement would then be made more precise by explaining that the fixed place of the citation in the prophetic speech is in *the development* of the accusation. Even where the reason for the announcement of judgment either begins the citation or consists of only a citation, this has the character of the development of an accusation. This means that behind the citation a direct accusation can be heard which simply establishes the fact of a transgression.

Scott also found this speech structure in the investigation of the speeches of Isaiah (*loc. cit.*, p. 180):

" The core of the reproach is a literally described com-

61

plaint, usually with one principal point and embodied in a single verse: ch. 5:20 f.; 7:13. In chs. 8:11-12, 10:1-22, and 28:7-8, this is expanded by a statement of the further consequences of the behavior condemned."

That Scott stressed another kind of development ("the further consequences of the behavior condemned") is beside the point here. The development of the accusation can be reduced to only a few types; the most frequent development is actually that of the citation.

With this more exact definition of the place of the citation in the whole of the prophetic speech, another important step toward the determination of its structure has been made. In my opinion Wolff's investigation has definitely shown that the function of the citation in the prophetic speech clearly proves its original unity as well as the distinguishableness of both parts.

A more recent work by H. W. Wolff should also be briefly examined here.

H. W. Wolff, " Hauptprobleme alttestamentlicher Prophetie," Ev. Theol., 1955, pp. 446–468

In Part I, Wolff approaches the problem from the viewpoint of the history of religion and particularly from that of the Mari letters, which will be mentioned later. The second part deals with the prophets' accounts of their call and the problem of ecstasy as it arises from them. With regard to understanding the prophetic *speeches* on the basis of ecstasy, Wolff raises the following objection:

"We have only third-person accounts about the genuine ecstatic in the Palestinian area. The prophet's own consciousness remains alert — the prophet *speaks* in the vision (Isa., ch. 6). The accounts depict a clear I-Thou relationship. The formation of the prophetic speech would remain incomprehensible from the viewpoint of ecstasy; the messenger's speech establishes an alert personal relationship to the surrounding world." (Pp. 455 f.)

It could also be added that not a trace of ecstasy can be found among the prophets in the Mari texts, as W. von Soden has noted. (See below.) The last comment by Wolff is the most important in my opinion, and can perhaps be outlined still more sharply. If it is correct that the prophetic speeches — or at least a large number of them — are composed and understood as speeches of messengers, it must be plainly stated that it is impossible for a message to be received in a state of ecstasy. Ecstatic experiences in the sphere of prophecy are, by all means, to be acknowledged. The messenger's speech, however, is to be clearly set apart from ecstasy. An alert and sensible ability to hear is the necessary presupposition at the moment the message (signified by the messenger formula, " Thus said Yahweh to me ") is received. Under certain circumstances ecstasy can precede it, or it can be found in the vicinity, but in no case may one assume that the reception of the messenger's speech occurred in ecstasy. That would contradict all that we know about the sending of the message and the style of the message in Israel herself and in the world surrounding her. By nature the messenger's speech is something different from an utterance received in ecstasy.

In Part III, " The Relation of Prophecy to the Old Israelitic Traditions," Wolff calls attention to the individual traditio-historical investigations on this theme. He shows that in spite of all the significance that the old Israelitic traditions had for prophecy, giving to it its reforming impulses, it still does not, as such, authorize or legitimate the speaking of the prophets. This is done by their call. Nevertheless, he is able to clarify the more exact determination of the multitude of traditional motifs in the prophetic proclamation:

" As spokesman for the lawsuit of Yahweh with Israel, as accuser in the name of Yahweh, the prophet leads the old history into the field; he creates his superior authority to accuse, not out of traditional knowledge, but . . . an-

63

nounces a new act of his God, and this action brings on the judgment."

Here also in this work by Wolff, one can see quite clearly that the prophetic speech is understood as a judgment-speech consisting of the accusation and announcement of judgment.

In Part IV, " Cult Prophecy," Wolff rejects the thesis of the Scandinavian school as going too far. Still we will have to ask " whether or not certain forms and materials of the prophetic proclamation must be understood considerably better from the viewpoint of the cult." He does not agree with the thesis of Würthwein that the prophetic judgment-speech could be understood as coming from a cultic event. One could, at the most, speak of imitations of the cultic form; one might sooner consider a direct cultic background for Deutero-Isaiah (von Waldow). " But even here one cannot say that a cultic institution supports the prophet, rather the prophet, manifesting a higher author-ity, supports and renews the worship orders of Israel in the shattering of cultic tradition." (P. 462.) The present sit-uation of the discussion of cult prophecy might permit two deductions:

1. " It is not possible to say that the writing prophets as a whole were cultic officials.

2. " It can no longer be claimed that the cult and proph-ecy are pure antitheses." (P. 446.)

EXCURSUS: THE TERMS " THREATENING-SPEECH "
AND " REPROACHING-SPEECH "

Since about the beginning of the century, the terms " threat-ening-speech " (Drohwort, or simply "threat") and " re-proaching-speech " (Scheltwort, or simply "reproach") have been common terms for the prophetic speeches. Insofar as I can tell, they are first encountered in the writings of Gunkel.[15]

Since the character of prophetic speech is already determined in a certain way by these terms, and since we now also stand at the beginning of the task of working through the prophetic speeches from a form-historical point of view,[16] a critical examination of these genre categories is worthwhile. Actually both are erroneous and it is almost inevitable that they lead to misunderstandings of the prophetic speech.

1. Threatening-speech: One senses an incongruity where the salvation- and judgment-speeches of the prophets are designated as promises and threats. While we understand "promise" as meaning an "announcement of salvation," the feeling of the linguistic idiom tells us that a threat does not, in a corresponding way, mean an announcement of doom. Indeed, a word that is an exact negative correspondence of *Verheissung* (promise) is not available in the German language; *Drohung* (threat), however, is scarcely suitable for this. A few instances might be mentioned which define this word:

(a) While we think at first of a word or word formation in connection with "promise," a threat can either be a word or a gesture or sometimes both. From our feeling for the language, one can even say that a threat still means primarily a threatening gesture or bearing: "And the winter still threatened with a terrifying countenance." The threatening word only comes secondarily.

(b) It is more significant, however, that "threat" in our linguistic usage, as well as in its early history, leaves open the question of the appearance of that which is threatened. The threatening of a man or a human community is something essentially different from the announcement of the doom that will overtake it. The disparity of the threat appears especially where the means used to threaten the other is named. If, e.g., during a war an opponent threatens to use poison gas, it is not the same as if he announces that he is going to use it. In this example the distinction between both concepts becomes obvious and generally understandable. It requires no further explanation.

(c) Another characteristic of the concept "threat" can be made clear by the last example. Quite often the threat has a qualified character. That means that the threatened use of poison gas has — stated or unstated — a condition in the background; e.g., if the opponent crosses over a defined line of de-

65

marcation, the poison gas will be put to use; the threat holds good in the event that . . .

(d) Another significant element of the threat is that it often stems directly from an insecure attitude or situation; it becomes an immediate necessity when the one making the threat is to some extent worried himself about his security. This is the reason (whether it is the bared teeth of a dog or the threatened use of poison gas) that one tends to make the threat terrifying in order to scare the other party, and also that one may run the risk of making himself more terrible than he actually is.

None of the four features suits the meaning of a prophetic announcement of judgment or doom.

(a) It is concerned exclusively with an event of speaking. Neither a threatening gesture nor appearance — of God or the prophet — is connected with it or intimated at any time. Insofar as a sign is connected with the announcement of judgment, this, as well, never even remotely resembles " teethbaring " or a showing of the means by which God threatens to execute his judgment.

(b) The announcement of judgment has the character of something settled: God has decided upon doom. The announcement itself is already a part of the sentence that has been decided upon by God. It is something essentially different from a threat.

(c) Because of this, the announcement also has an unqualified character. It holds good not merely in the case of . . . , but it actually puts the forthcoming judgment into motion, even if the prophets are not the ones who execute the judgment.[17]

(d) The announcement of judgment in prophecy presupposes the unqualified Lordship of God in history and over history. It is an expression of this sovereignty that God causes a judgment which he has concluded to be announced. A mere threat could certainly have adversely affected this sovereignty.

This shows that the announcement is something essentially different from the threat and that this conception (whether one says threatening-speech [Drohrede], threat [Drohung], or threatening-word [Drohwort]) is unsuitable as a designation

66

of the prophetic judgment message. Another important argument based on the character of prophetic speech as a messenger's speech can be added. A threat is transmitted very poorly by a messenger. It is certainly possible, but a threat is unsuited for transmission through a messenger. By nature, the threat is connected with a gesture or attitude that cannot be effectively mediated by a messenger. Directness is essential to it. And, indeed, the prophetic speeches which have been passed down to us as messengers' speeches, actually do not have the character of a threat. The prophets do not threaten. They say what is already decided and will come.

This does not exclude the possibility that the prophetic announcement of judgment is capable of appropriating elements of the threat or threatening-speech. Neither should it be denied that in many cases the announcement of judgment can have much in common with or be closely connected with a threat. That the announcement, by nature, is not a threat, however, can also be shown in a comparison. A very distinct form of a genuine threat is found in the Old Testament in the threats of the transgressor against the pious man in the Psalms of Lament of the individual. Even if the threats of the transgressor here are only intimated and stylized, the essential distinction from the prophetic announcement of judgment is evident.

The designation — announcement of judgment (*Gerichtsankündigung*) or announcement of ill (*Unheilsankündigung*) — which I have used instead of this is not new. It is and already has been used for a long while by a number of investigators and thus requires no special justification. A simple word corresponding to *Verheissung* (promise) is not available in German, so a compound word corresponding to *Heilsankündigung* (announcement of salvation) must be used.[18]

2. Reproaching-speech: With this term the situation is possibly even clearer. It fails to convey the intended meaning. Indeed, even more important here is the presupposition of whether both parts of the prophetic judgment-speech are generally independent, or whether they only comprise a prophetic speech when they are together. To call the part of the prophetic speech which provided the reason for the announcement a " reproach " is meaningful only upon the presupposi-

67

tion that it can exist completely independent of the announcement.

Then the reproach is an event that is completely independent within itself. The practice of joining reproaches and threats together into a unified structure, which is so frequent in the prophets, would itself be highly remarkable. Naturally, one can reproach and threaten in one breath, but how and why should a whole develop out of these two? If, however, the " reproaching-speech " is recognized as the reason for the threatening-speech (as in Balla, e.g.) , can a threat be grounded upon a reproach (insult) ? If the connection of both parts of the prophetic speech is recognized and if this connection is taken seriously, then the term, " reproaching-speech " has already become superfluous (as in H. W. Wolff) .

Apart from this connection, consideration should be given to whether the part of the prophetic speech that gives the reason should be called a reproach. What does it mean to reproach?

(a) Reproaching is actually a sterilized and domesticated form of cursing or exorcising. That cannot be supported and developed in detail here; a few observations must suffice. In German the origin of the insult in the curse is still clearly recognizable though it no longer happens directly but indirectly. From " Confound you! " (*Verflucht du!*) or " Curse you! " (*Fluch dir*) or the like, has come: " You damned lout! " (*Du verdammter Lausejunge!*) and others. The many animal names used in reproaching still serve as one of the best reminders of the curse which turns one into a beast (fables) . In English the words " He called me names " say the same thing.

(b) The threatening charge, " What kind of idiotic thing have you done again? Such a crazy thing! " is something else. We have in German a very distinctive concept for that: *jemanden heruntermachen* (to lay someone low) . In this " laying low " the same thing happens as in the " laying low " of the reproaching-speech. In both kinds of reproaching, the directness of the speech — the immediacy of the reproaching address — is decisive. One cannot reproach through a messenger. Either the messenger himself would then have to become the one reproaching, or it is just no longer a reproach. For this reason it is already obvious that a messenger's speech cannot be a reproach.

68

Now something must be added that goes deeper. As a derivative of the curse, the reproach comes out of the magical understanding of existence. A curse is *directly* effective, and the same is also basically true of the reproach (cf. Matt. 5:22).

Then the prophetic accusation cannot be a reproach. It is certainly not concerned with reproaching, but with establishing the facts just as the evidence is established in court proceedings and then " laid to the charge " of the accused. In the development of this accusation prophetic speech also *can* occasionally appropriate elements of the reproach. Reproaching-speeches are encountered and occasionally even an angry, reproaching " laying low " (as that ever and again intrudes itself into the court proceedings). The reproach, however, always remains secondary — adjunctive. One has no right to call this entire substantiating part of the prophetic judgment-speech a reproaching-speech.

Moreover, I do not propose a new term here, but only plead for one already used by many investigators. If one wants this part of the prophetic speech to be *a part,* i.e., to designate its function in the prophetic speech as a whole, then the formal term " reason " (*Begründung*) is completely sufficient. If, however, one wants to express what this reason consists of — what it, in and of itself, represents — then the term " accusation " (*Anklage*) is appropriate. Of course one must then make allowance for the fact that the term " accusation " has a broader meaning here than the mere judicial one, and must further allow that the same term also designates something entirely different, namely, a structural member of the lament in the Psalms of Lamentation — the " accusation of God." [19]

The distinction lies in the fact that God is the object in the " accusation of God " in The Psalms, whereas in the prophetic accusation he is the subject. That the same term appears in both of these entirely different places is not altogether accidental — it is for good reason. As a matter of fact, one sees that in the speech form of the judgment-speeches in Deutero-Isaiah,[20] both can be found next to each other in contrast. This is particularly true in Isa. 43:22-28, where the accusation that the people in exile make against God is opposed by the accusation of God (subj.). The content completely justifies this usage of the term "accusation " in both of these originally quite different places.

The term "accusation" for the substantiating part of the prophetic judgment-speech has the advantage of being able to express well and clearly the differentiation of this part of the speech. One can distinguish between the social, the cultic, the theological, and the personal accusation.

With the terms "announcement of judgment," "reason," and "accusation," a decision about the understanding of the prophetic speeches so designated has also, of course, taken place. This definitely draws them into a certain proximity to the court procedure. That which happens in these speeches between God and his people (through the mediation of the messenger) can be seen in the manner or structure of a court action. Corresponding to this would be the many speeches of the prophets in which the court situation is unambiguously indicated and described. In addition to that, however, it would be presupposed that the content of that which is announced to the people of God by the messenger should be understood essentially as an act of the judgment of God upon his people. This is what H. W. Wolff said in the sentence cited above. Pointing in the same direction is the work of H. J. Boecker, *Redeformen des israelitischen Rechtslebens* (diss., Bonn, 1959), particularly pp. 145 ff.

13. E. Würthwein, " Amos-Studien," ZAW 62 (1949/50), pp. 10–52

Even if this study does not have anything to do with speech forms directly, it is still especially important for our question. After a short review of the articles by S. Mowinckel, H. Junker, A. R. Johnson, and A. Haldar, which have proved the existence and significance of cult prophecy in Israel, Würthwein inquires into the relation of the writing prophets to this institution. He is correct in saying at the outset that this question cannot be answered in a general way. Since the situation was different with each prophet, it will always have to be answered by consulting the text. He raises the question in relation to the prophet Amos. In a discussion of the article by H. H. Rowley,

" Was Amos a *Nābî'?*" (Eissfeldt *Festschrift,* 1947, pp. 191–198), Würthwein works out a valuable exegesis of Amos 7:10-17. He says that Amos does not oppose being addressed as a *nābî';* v. 14 is related to the past of the prophet and Amos advances the claim that his vocation as a (salvation) *nābî'* might continue even if he is *now* under the commission of Yahweh to announce judgment. The situation is thus explained best by saying that the entire prophecy of Amos is judgment prophecy, though the content of the oracles against the foreign nations is that of a salvation-speech for Israel. (Würthwein maintains that Amos 9:8 did not originate with Amos.) Both of the first visions of Amos show him as just such a salvation prophet. As an intercessor he seeks to bring about salvation for his people. In these complexes Amos is actually a salvation prophet and the fact that they stand next to one another in The Book of Amos is best explained as a temporal succession. Amos was first a salvation prophet and was called to be such, but then he became a judgment prophet and the visions still clearly reflect this change. This is also the reason that ch. 7:10-17 is the only first-person account by the prophet; Amos must struggle for his right to appear as a prophet with this new message.

In a second section Würthwein asks whether there was a tradition to which this judgment prophecy could have joined. He shows that the accusations that Amos advances — above all, the social accusations — are based upon the demands of the preexilic law in Israel: " Amos refers back to the amphictyonic law in the awareness that the demands of the old Yahweh amphictyony are still binding." Yahweh answers the violation of these demands with the abrogation of the covenant; that means the announcement of judgment. The accusation, therefore, does not come out of a general ethical consciousness, or a moral or social fervor, but out of the spirit of Yahwistic religion. " The great, fundamental thoughts of the Yahwistic faith are already present. Amos has proclaimed to his contemporaries that their obligatory character still exists and that disobedience in everyday life means decline and death." (P. 52.) [20a]

For that reason this study is particularly important for the inquiry into the prophetic speech forms, since here — so far as I can see for the first time — an early salvation prophecy in Israel (in Amos in the oracles against the nations and in his intercessory office in which he intended to bring about salvation) is quite clearly distinguished from a later salvation prophecy. (Note 60, p. 39: " I maintain that ch. 9:8ab-15 is not genuine; compare particularly the arguments by S. Mowinckel, *Psalmstudien V* (1921), pp. 266 f."; this decision by Würthwein can only mean that a kind of salvation prophecy is expressed in ch. 9:8ab-15, which belongs to a later time.) The *nābī'* of the early period, *before* and during the time of the writing prophets, was a salvation prophet by virtue of his office (also according to Johnson, cult prophecy *is* salvation prophecy) ; he had to bring about salvation for his people and this took place in connection with or in the milieu of the cult. During the first period of his activity Amos belonged to these *neḇī'îm*, and only then became a judgment prophet. Chapter 9:8ab-15, another type of salvation-speech from a later time, would then have been joined to the collection of his speeches later — most probably in the Judaistic phase of its tradition. Two important observations for the history of the prophetic speech thus are encountered here.

1. The prophetic salvation-speech had a history. Such oracles against the nations as Amos 1:3 to 2:5 belong to an early phase of the salvation-speech and are actually indirect salvation-speeches for Israel. It should also be added here that we find the very same thing in the collection of speeches out of the Syro-Ephraimite War in the early period of Isaiah. It is particularly clear in the salvation-speech to Ahaz (ch. 7:1 ff.) , which is uttered in the form of an announcement of doom for the enemies of Jerusalem. In addition, the function of the prophet as intercessor belongs in this early period of salvation prophecy. The milieu of the

72

intercessory speech is clearly the service of worship — it is not actually prophetic speech (it belongs in proximity to the " Priestly salvation-oracle " which was combined with the prophetic speech in Deutero-Isaiah). On the other hand, the prophetic salvation-speech such as the kind found in Amos 9:8 ff. belongs to a later phase. It is improbable that this type of salvation prophecy was found in the time of Amos or earlier.

2. Judgment prophecy is located in the middle between an earlier and a later phase of salvation prophecy. It has its own allotted time. One can vigorously agree with Würthwein that the change in the prophecy of Amos — if such is to be accepted — is determined by a change in the attitude of God to his people. The silencing of Amos' intercession attests to the new situation now appearing. God has decided upon doom for his people and Amos must now be his messenger. Judgment prophecy extends from this point to the execution of judgment, first upon Israel and then upon Judah. Its time comes between these two points. For this reason one can also agree with Würthwein in that he has seen that the assimilation of the salvation prophecy from the earlier nābî'-period of Amos means that prophecies of salvation and doom are not basically exclusive, but rather, that both have their time. It was *the same God* in whose name Amos at first acted in word and intercession to bring about salvation for his nation and then proclaimed judgment.[21]

The structure of the prophetic speech as an announcement of doom is rooted in this temporal and historical limitation of the prophetic judgment-speech which was formed for a specific period. That appears particularly clear in the work of Würthwein. He understands and clearly defines the prophetic judgment-speech as a unity having two parts.

" The judgment-speeches of Amos contain these two elements — the irrational announcement of judgment and the rational grounds for it. The prophet knows about the judg-

73

ment through the revelation which has been imparted to him alone. For this reason the announcement of judgment is usually given in a speech of Yahweh, while the grounds for it are given by the prophet himself." (P. 41.)

He shows that this is exactly the case in the exegesis of ch. 7:10-17 (pp. 22 f.) : " The problem of vs. 14b-16 is to give the reason in advance for v. 17. It is frequent in the prophets, and particularly in Amos (H. W. Wolff), for the reason to be given in the form of a declaratory sentence with the threat joined to it by *lākēn*. Typical also is the distinct separation between the threatening-speech of God to which it refers and the speech of the prophet (H. W. Wolff). In vs. 14-16 the guilt of Amaziah should be established so that the ill which is announced to him appears to be inwardly justified."

That which confirms our previous investigation may be stated here:

1. The precise verification of the function of the prophetic judgment-speech in contrast to the salvation-speech (which precedes it temporally) shows that both parts of this speech *necessarily* belong together and that here it is not a question of an independent " threatening-speech " or " scolding," but rather, of an announcement of judgment.

2. Following the work of H. W. Wolff completely at this point, Würthwein very accurately sees the distinction between both parts of the prophetic word of judgment *qua* word of God. Only the announcement of judgment, strictly speaking, is the word of God revealed to him which he has to pass on. In the reason, the prophet himself speaks.[21a] Whether the distinction made by the concepts " rational " (for the reason) and " irrational " (for the announcement) is appropriate or not, may be left undecided. Certainly from the viewpoint of Würthwein, who is concerned with working out the particularity of the prophetic announcement of judgment against the background of cult prophecy, this confirmation of H. W. Wolff's observations is notable and important. Würthwein, however, now significantly supple-

74

ments the previously acquired understanding with a discussion of the reason — thus of the prophetic accusation — thereby giving it an important complement (p. 41):

" It can be shown in both of the major themes of the accusations of Amos . . . that he advocated no independent ethos of his own making. Weiser has already pointed out . . . ' that in regard to content, the ethical position which must be presupposed in the criticism of the prophets does not at any point go beyond the moral guiding principles which were already known in Israel before Amos.' (P. 316.)

" One must go still farther, however, and forthrightly assert that in his criticism, Amos is closely and concretely dependent on the religious traditions of his people. (P. 41.)

" With his accusation oriented to the Book of the Covenant, Amos goes back to the amphictyonic law in the awareness that the orders and demands of the old Yahweh amphictyony were still valid for Israel. With her deeds Israel has not transgressed some imaginary moral law, but has become guilty before the concrete demands of the law of her God. Amos presumes this law to be well-known." (P. 49.)

The prophetic accusation thus takes on a different character indeed from what it had in the prophetic exegesis which was based on an unhistorical individualistic-idealstic concept of ethics (Wellhausen, Duhm, and even Gunkel). This prophetic accusation is thereby shown to be an event that is understandable only as a part of a definite history, and as an event that was dependent on this history. Just as the announcement of judgment had its time— as was said above — so it is linked with the preceding epoch and cannot be understood apart from it: linked with the " covenant," which on one side was God's election, and on the other side the nation's covenantal obligations.[22]

Only this historical rootage of the prophetic accusation enables its characteristic connection with the announcement of judgment to be completely explained. In ground-

75

ing the announced intervention of God *against* his people, the " therefore " in " therefore thus said Yahweh " connects the accusation to which it is joined with that which was the real basis of the accusation, namely, the disregard of the deeds of God experienced by Israel in her history which established her existence as a nation. While the announcement of judgment actually announces something new and *therefore* is in a real sense a repetition of that which was revealed to the prophet, the reason for this announcement, the accusation, rests on the will of God which was already revealed and proclaimed to the people a long while before, and to which the people had *now* answered with consummate disobedience.

In the " Amos-Studien," Würthwein clarified a few important points concerning the relation of cult prophecy = salvation prophecy and judgment prophecy. Corresponding to the emphasis of the text, this has produced more results related to judgment prophecy, which completely predominates in Amos, than to salvation prophecy of which only traces are recognizable. There are still questions remaining. First of all, if Würthwein says on p. 34 that Amos " in his own consciousness never ceased being a *nābî'*," and that because of this he did not separate himself from his office as a judgment prophet, what does that mean in regard to the speeches of the prophets? How or in what sense is he still a *nābî'* if the office of the *nābî'* consists of speaking words of salvation? In Würthwein's opinion *only* judgment-speeches have been passed down to us since Amos' change. Was he also in a cultic office as a judgment prophet? Since in this article Würthwein does not go into this question, one must conclude from it that nothing can be discerned in the texts of this epoch — either of Amos' work as a salvation prophet or of the cultic function of Amos as a judgment prophet.

This question is taken up in another article:

76

E. Würthwein, " Der Ursprung der prophetischen Gerichtsrede," ZThK 49 (1952), pp. 1–15

In this article Würthwein goes a step beyond the previous work. While he was directly concerned in the " Amos-Studien " with clearly contrasting both materially and temporally the activity of Amos as a cult = salvation prophet with the activity of Amos as a judgment prophet,[23] he asks in the later article whether or not a connection might also be perceived between the speeches of the judgment prophet and cultic events; that means, therefore, whether or not judgment prophecy is more closely related to the cult than it was previously believed to be, and also than he himself saw in his earlier article.

Proceeding from this question, he finds the origin of a small group of speeches, termed " prophetic judgment-speeches " by Gunkel, in a cultic event — an act of the cultic drama — in which Yahweh appears as a judge. The texts which he cites are Hos. 4:1 f.; 12:3 f.; Isa. 3:13 f.; Micah 6:1 ff.; Jer. 2:5 ff.; 25:30 ff.; Mal. 3:5. Gunkel had defined them as reproaches that had been couched in the form of the judgment-speech in the same way that the prophets had borrowed other speech forms. It does not seem correct to Würthwein to say that the prophetic speeches in which Yahweh voices the accusation through the mouth of the prophet representing him are imitations of the profane judgment-speeches. He finds the allusion to the original place of prophetic judgment-speeches in a group of texts in The Psalms in which Yahweh appears as a judge (Ps. 96:11-13; 98:7-9; 76:8-10; 50:1-7). He must, however, allow the question concerning the particular feast with which this appearance of God as judge was connected to remain open, as well as the extent to which the prophetic judgment-speeches were actually spoken in the cult. He does mean, however, that this cultic act might be the origin, not only of that small group of texts named at first,

77

but even more " that generally, our thesis is also of significance for the reproaching-speech." This means that it must be asked whether or not the prophetic reproaching-speech has in general grown entirely out of the cultic judgment-speech.

This last, merely suggested expansion of the thesis of the article is very risky because only the passages containing the true prophetic " judgment-speech," cited at first by Würthwein, are corroborated by the texts. But even in these texts the basis of agreement is quite narrow. When Würthwein (p. 15) says, " What is more obvious than to connect them with one another, i.e., to derive the prophetic judgment-speech from the cult as well as the judgment-speech in The Psalms? " then it must be noticed by way of qualification that no judgment-*speeches* at all are present in the Psalm texts which he cites. It only says in these passages in The Psalms, *that* God comes to judge; accusation-speeches by God however, i.e., that which should actually be comparable, occur in none of these Psalms. The very word *rîb*, correctly rendered by Würthwein with " accuse," and designated by him as a characteristic verb, is also not found anywhere in the Psalm texts.

What is more important, however, is that Würthwein, in the " Amos-Studien," had perceived the prophetic judgment-speech as a whole having two parts — the announcement of doom and its reason, the accusation — and had significantly clarified it by his investigation. In this new article only the one part, which Würthwein here calls a " reproaching-speech " (the term was never used in his earlier article), is taken into consideration and this is treated as an independent self-contained speech form. Here an unmistakable tension exists between the two articles. In my opinion, the structure of the prophetic speech in the " Amos-Studien " is apprehended with greater precision and in greater correspondence to the text than here, where basically the structure of the prophetic speech has completely given way to an *idea* that is encountered in it, namely, the

78

idea of the judging God. If common ground (between the prophetic and the Psalm texts) is sought, it is found only in this idea. The speech forms are not important for that. Here, however, a certain lack of sharpness appears in the comparison. This can be seen in the fact that the addressee of the speech can change. Whether Yahweh speaks judgment to Israel or to the nations is not important for the cultic idea or the cultic act, and so the addressee in the text changes any number of times. That Würthwein is comparing only the idea can be seen especially in the fact that he cites the whole textual unit, i.e., the complete prophetic speech, only part of the time, and at other times he names only the verses that tell of the accusation. In the texts selected in this manner, Würthwein finds a structure having two parts. An introductory announcement is:

Yahweh has a *rîb* . . .

Yahweh appears *lārîb* . . .

The accusation itself follows (in the second or third person). The structure proves to be correct for Isa. 1:18-20; 3:12-15; and Micah 6:1-5; however, in a passage such as Isa. 5:1-7, which clearly reflects a judicial process, the sentence, i.e., the judge's verdict or the announcement of judgment, is added and clearly forms a unity with the accusation. Also in Ezek. 4:1 ff. (a passage cited by Würthwein), the announcement of judgment follows in v. 3, being connected by *'al kēn;* in Jer. 2:5 ff. as well, it follows in v. 9; in Jer. 25:30 ff. no explicit accusation is contained at all, only the announcement of judgment.

The result that clearly emerges from this is that there is a structure in which two parts, the accusation and the announcement of judgment, follow the introduction: the structure therefore which Würthwein had worked out in his " Amos-Studien " as being characteristic of the prophetic announcement of doom. One then may not isolate a part — the accusation — as if it were an independent speech form whose origin could be sought separately. In any case one must be careful about conclusions that are

79

based on a definition of this isolated part alone.

Würthwein's both valuable and important conclusion in the " Amos-Studien " — that the speeches of Amos as a cult or salvation *nābî'* are to be clearly and unmistakably distinguished from the speeches of Amos as a judgment prophet — is immediately threatened with being obliterated again if in the later article, the speeches of the judgment prophets should be proved to have grown out of a cultic event and to belong to it.

One can agree with Würthwein that the " prophetic judgment-speeches " with which he begins are certainly related to the speech of God as a judge. Such speech is widespread in the whole Old Testament and found especially in The Psalms. The judging action of God is encountered throughout a great breadth of writings, from the earliest to the latest, in very different kinds of contexts. This does not commend a strict separation between a profane and sacral legal action. In ancient times in which all areas of life ultimately rested on an order regulated by the cult (von Rad, *Theology I,* Eng. ed., p. 32) one can hardly speak of a purely profane legal process that had no relation to God. Yahweh is appealed to as a judge (" May Yahweh judge between you and me ") , he is called upon as a witness, is sworn by, and in an ordeal, he is the one who decides the disputed issue. Thus when the prophets of the eighth and seventh centuries allowed Yahweh to appear before his people as an accuser, when he makes an accusation against his people in the word of the prophets, Yahweh acts in accordance with his most distinctive nature — he provides justice. It is not necessary for this to have a special origin in the cultic drama. The particular prophetic situation in which God appears as an accuser against his own people certainly does not correspond to the office of the cult prophet whose problem is, according to Würthwein's " Amos-Studien," to bring about salvation in the cult for his people.

It is very difficult to trace the history of the investigation of the prophetic speech forms. It has certainly been done only fragmentarily in the foregoing work because heretofore there has been no continuity in it; there has been either quite different, individual initiatory works or an uncritical appropriation of earlier conclusions. So an attempt must be made to summarize the previous gains, at least in their most important features.

At the beginning stands the observation that was first made in regard to the preliterary prophets and then was found to be true of the prophets generally: we are dealing in prophecy with a collection of *individual* prophetic sayings.[24]

In the introduction by Steuernagel (1921) the major forms of prophetic speech had already appeared: the accusation directed to their own people and the announcement of judgment. From the religio-historical viewpoint, prophetic speech was considered to be close to simple, primitive forms of speech (for Hölscher, the incantation); the rhythmic form of these speeches was discovered (Hölscher). Gunkel exposed the diversity of the prophetic speech forms, making it possible to distinguish the few original prophetic genres from the many forms of speech that were borrowed from other areas (such as songs of all kinds, Priestly Torah, judgment-speeches, and others). This distinction, as such, has found general acceptance, but Gunkel's work could not yet explain what the genuine prophetic speech forms were. The same reason could be given for the lack of success of Gressmann's suggestion (which was influenced a great deal by Gunkel) that the combined salvation- and judgment-speech comes at the beginning and that its two parts would have separated when salvation and judgment prophecy came to oppose each other (as is seen in I Kings, ch. 22). In his very stimulating and consequen-

81

tial investigation, however, he did raise the question concerning the historical relation of salvation and judgment prophecy.

A new section in the history of the investigation of the prophetic speech forms began with the discovery that the prophetic speeches were passed down to us as messenger's speeches, in the style of a message. It was made almost simultaneously by Lindblom and Köhler independent of each other. Lindblom investigates the (later so-called) "messenger formula," "Thus said the Lord," and finds out that it is exclusively characteristic of prophetic literature, and for that reason must express something fundamental about it. He finds its origin in the proclamation formula of the monarchs and in the Ancient Near Eastern message style. From its history within prophecy he can draw conclusions about the history of prophecy itself. This represents the first investigation of an individual prophetic speech form that illuminates the correct path for later research to follow.

L. Köhler goes beyond J. Lindblom in that he explains, on the basis of the form of the messenger's speech, that the prophetic speech as such, and as a whole, is a messenger's speech (Isa., ch. 6). He uses the sending of a messenger in the secular realm as an illustration of its setting in life. In this way Köhler gave a new foundation for the investigation of the prophetic speech in its character as a messenger's speech. But if prophetic speech as a whole is a messenger's speech, the question arises of whether this message character is seen only in its framework or in its content as well. Wildberger's investigation, which follows the path of Lindblom and Köhler, was limited to the investigation of the framework. This question, however, is still undecided.

Investigations into individual prophetic writings (Balla: Amos; Scott: Isaiah; Wildberger: Jeremiah), though not yet concurring in the definition of the prophetic speech as a messenger's speech, do take a significant step forward. They proceed from Gunkel's division of the specific prophetic speeches into threats and reproaches. Almost without exception Balla finds threatening-speeches with a reason (= reproach) in the units ascertained in Amos. Scott finds that they stand combined in most places and can also plainly state that *one* oracle includes a censure and a threat. Both, therefore, come very close to the insight that the real unity within prophetic speech is the prophetic judgment-speech consisting of an announcement of judgment and reason.

Balla goes on to make important observations on the relation of both of these parts to each other. The announcement of doom, he notes, is in many cases the true word of God, and the reason, on the other hand, is more the word of the prophet. In this connection he sees that the emphasis that originally lay entirely on the " threat " can be moved to the reason.

Scott, in that he understands the kernel of the " reproach " to be an accusation, finds a structure that completely determines this part. The short accusation, which usually consists of one sentence, is expanded by sentences that show the consequences of the guilt. He finds likewise, a two-membered structure in the other part — the announcement. The doom might be literally depicted at the outset and then illustrated in pictorial concepts.

In considering the question of the prehistory of prophetic speech, Balla finds a completely different form known as the seer's speech (I Kings 22:17). The work of Wildberger on Jeremiah distinguishes itself from both of those just mentioned in that he limits himself to the investigation of the framework, and therefore, to the formulas that enclose the single prophetic speeches. In doing so he comes to such important distinctions as the distinction made between the personal account of the prophet (*Selbstbericht*) and the account in the third person (*Fremdbericht*), which exhibit different speech forms. The distinction he makes between the messenger's formula — *kô 'āmar yhwh* — and the introductory formula, is also important

83

since he shows that the messenger formula actually belongs to the speech of Yahweh. The work of Wildberger also shows, however, that the investigation of the framework cannot be separated from that of the content without harm. The leading question of his work, How are the word of Yahweh and the word of the prophet related in the prophetic utterances that have been passed down to us? cannot be answered without the observations which Balla and Scott have made of the character of the prophetic speech as *such*, completely apart from the enclosing formulas. If, as Wildberger has correctly seen, the messenger formula actually belongs to the speech of Yahweh, it can only be explained on the basis of the structure of the speech in which it stands. The observations of Balla and Scott then come close to the realization that the messenger formula was not originally the introduction of the *whole* prophetic speech, as Wildberger believed, but was rather the introduction of the announcement, as Balla observed it in a majority of the cases in Amos.

In his *Althebraischen Literatur*, Hempel gives the most important comprehensive description of prophetic speech since Gunkel and in doing so seeks to arrive at a history of the prophetic oracle. Gunkel's thesis that the very short saying stands at the beginning is adopted and developed farther by Hempel. This short utterance is God speaking in the divine " I." Hempel sees the closeness of this speech of God to the messenger-speech and the herald's call, but does not give it the same significance as Köhler and Lindblom. Hempel also retains Gunkel's basic division of the prophetic speech into the threat and reproach. It is now more evident in his work, however, that one can no longer maintain that two basic forms such as these are independent units. Hempel shows that the real prophetic oracle is the announcement that is proclaimed in the style of the speech of God and is introduced with either the divine oath or the messenger formula. The reason is an addition made by the prophet — a " primary rationalization." Next

84

to this "primary rationalization" Hempel finds a "secondary" one in the expression of the personal involvement of the prophet in the exhortation, warning, and cry of woe. With the subjective embellishments, which also include the different formulations of the speech (introductory formulas) and the formal elements, appears the influence of foreign style forms that cause the composition to become more and more extensive.

While Gunkel saw only the great diversity of prophetic speech forms in all of this, it seems to me that Hempel has correctly recognized that two major levels must be distinguished in the structure of the prophetic speeches and that, therefore, the warning and exhortation are not to be placed next to the announcement of judgment but after it. Corresponding to this, Hempel, in his classification of the prophetic speeches under the heading he calls "predicative speeches," distinguishes the warning, reproach, repentance-speech, and the conditional promise from the "unconditional" — the threat, reproach, and salvation-speech — and explains that the former, in contrast to the latter, are secondary. It can only be added that Hempel's arrangement of the threat next to the salvation-speech does not fully correspond to his own description since he has correctly recognized that the reproach serving as the reason originally belongs with the threat serving as the announcement.

Hempel's remarks about the nature of the word of God are important for this observation (p. 58): "Where divinity declares its future-determining will, the threatened or promised fate has already become an unalterable reality through such a declaration (the prophetic perfect)." This establishes, namely, that "at an earlier time the threat and reproach are to be distinguished from the speech of God and the prophet." Because of the efficacious character of the word of God, the proclaimed word must be God's word directly, while the reason that is joined to it can be only indirectly the word of God.

In Balla, Scott, and Hempel, we found striking agree-

85

ment upon the emerging understanding of a basic form of the prophetic judgment-speech which has two parts both by nature, and in regard to its origin. In this view, the actual word of God which is spoken by the prophet represents the announcement of judgment. An appropriate accusation is attached to this as the reason. The clear formulation of this observation was hindered by the classification of the two independent genres, the reproach and threat, on a par with each other; but it is stated clearly by H. W. Wolff. From the outset he deals with the reason as a part of a compound whole which consists of a " speech about the future " (*Zukunftswort*) and the reason. At the same time he finds that the " normal form " — the reason as a declaratory sentence — is joined to the threat with *lākēn* or something similar. He completes this by defining the relationship of both parts to each other; here he agrees with what Hempel said about this (both of these works appear in the same year — 1934), i.e., the real messenger's speech is the announcement, and the reason is essentially the word of the prophet himself.

In the publication *Das Zitat im Prophetenspruch* (1937), Wolff supported both aspects of this thesis and developed one aspect by means of a more exact definition of the part that gives the reason. In this work the understanding of the prophetic speech as a messenger's speech is more strongly in evidence. This means that the earlier way of interpreting the prophetic speech from the viewpoint of a prophetic experience is quite consciously relinquished. The prophet is neither a mystic (Lindblom), nor a giver of oracles (Hölscher), nor an ecstatic (Hölscher and many others). The definition of the prophetic speech as a messenger's speech results in a confirmation of the primary relation of the announcement and reason: " From the outset the judgment is set forth with a reason," moreover, " the saying which is solely concerned with showing the future is . . . actually unprophetic." *Further effort at gaining an understanding of the prophetic speech forms must, in*

86

my opinion, begin with this new definition of the pro-
phetic judgment-speech as a messenger's speech consisting
of two parts, the reason and the announcement.

The intention of the works that have appeared since is
not the investigation of prophetic speech forms. The question of the relation of prophecy to the cult had acquired a
fascinating attraction. This question was pursued in two directions: (a) the specific origin of prophetic speech and
also prophetic speech forms in the cult was investigated
(e.g., Engnell, Würthwein); (b) the relation of the prophetic speech to the traditions that were carried on by the
cult was investigated (particularly in the dissertation by
E. Rohland, " Die Bedeutung der Erwählungstraditionen
Israels für die Eschatologie der AT-lichen Propheten,"
Heidelberg, 1956, Microcopy).

So far as I can see, the inquiry with which we are concerned here, i.e., the inquiry into the prophetic speech
forms, was not furthered in either of these directions.
H. W. Wolff also sees this in his article of 1955; he finds
that the work on prophecy which has subsequently been
done in the two directions just mentioned neither continues nor fundamentally opposes the definition he gave of
the prophetic judgment-speech.

In addition, may I say that clear and well-founded conclusions can be reached along these two paths only if the
results of the investigation into the forms of prophetic
speech which were reached through long and painstaking
work are noticed and further developed. It seems to me
that a comparison of both of Würthwein's works can be
particularly instructive in this regard.

These works indicate a new phase in the prophetic investigation. It is introduced through the discovery of cult
prophecy in Israel and the resulting question that arises
concerning the relation of the writing prophets to this cult
prophecy. At the beginning of his article of 1949/50,
Würthwein refers briefly to the Scandinavian and English
research on cult prophecy. The results of this research do

not need to concern us here because the question of speech forms does not come up in all of these works. In contrast to this, the work of Würthwein stands entirely within the tradition of research oriented toward the study of the history of forms. *In his work the questions concerning the relation of the writing prophets to the cult come together with the question about the effect of such a relationship upon the speech forms.*

Würthwein answers the question of whether or not Amos was a cult prophet through a temporal stratification of his speeches. Amos was a salvation prophet (and as such, a cult prophet), as shown by the oracles against the foreign nations and the visions. Then, however, he became a cult prophet as his remaining speeches show. What Würthwein says about the judgment-speeches of Amos is a full confirmation of the essential thesis of H. W. Wolff concerning the prophetic judgment-speech. Regarding salvation prophecy, the work of Würthwein brings about the important separation of the early and late salvation-speeches in the prophetic tradition. But most important of all, Würthwein makes a sharp distinction between the forms of the judgment-speech which have *nothing* to do with the cult, and the salvation-speeches which stem from cultic procedures and institutions, or at least are related to them.

This is basically different in the article of 1952. Here the understanding that the speeches of Amos, the cult-*nābî'*, are to be temporally and materially distinguished from the speeches of Amos, the judgment prophet, is abandoned. Instead of this, he wants to show that the speeches of the judgment prophets have grown out of and belong to a cultic event, namely, an act of the cult drama in which Yahweh appears as a judge. Without any decision about this thesis here, let it only be stated that this question carries no significance for the investigation of the prophetic speech forms. The structure of the prophetic speech gives way here to an idea found in his work which made it nec-

88

essary to surrender the unity of the prophetic speech that he understood correctly in the article of 1949/50, and to deal with the " reproach " again as an independent unit.

Once again we should note the article by H. W. Wolff in 1937. In this article Wolff always describes the event that is reflected in the prophetic judgment-speech as a judicial proceeding, or " dispute," or process. Concerning this he says, for example: " The legal procedure is the stylistic background of the prophetic citations," or, " One of the origins of the citation is the judicial life "; and other similar statements occur often. (This is worked out in the commentary on Hosea, e.g., in Hos. 4:1-3.) Of course, that only corresponds to the usual terminology: prophetic judgment-speech or prophetic accusation. For this reason it seems to me to be fully understandable that a group of these speeches are worded in the language of judicial proceedings. That corresponds to the nature of the genre as a whole. Is it still necessary to accept the origin of this genre in a cultic event that is still undiscovered?

B. A Survey

I. THE SPEECH FORMS
IN THE PROPHETIC BOOKS

After the discussion of the previous work on the prophetic speech forms, the positive gains from this critical analysis should now be described. In so doing only an outline can be offered. The following sketch makes no claim to completeness, but only intends to fill in the major lines of prophetic speech forms proceeding from the whole to the individual parts.

As it was shown in the discussion of Wilderberger's study, the prophetic books contain three major kinds of speech: (A) accounts, (B) prophetic speeches, (C) utterances directed from man to God (prayer). These three major forms are distributed very differently in the prophetic books. A few books (Micah; Isa., chs. 40 to 55; 56 to 66; Nahum; Hab.; Zeph.; Mal.) do not contain any accounts; Jonah consists only of an account (prophetic legend); and likewise, the prophecy before Amos is passed down only in accounts (in the historical books).[1]

The major component of most prophetic books is the prophetic speech, i.e., the words of God delivered by a messenger of God. They can be very different in their own form as well as in their framework. What makes it into a prophetic speech can only be seen by surveying the whole

90

stock of prophetic speeches in the Old Testament as well as the parallels from other religions, so far as there are such.

The third component represents the utterances within the prophetic books that are directed from man to God. At the outset they must be sharply separated from the prophetic speeches in regard to their genre. They have the character of the *reactio,* the answer. Their two major forms are (as in The Psalms) lament and praise.

In The Book of Jeremiah, for example, the " lament of the individual " is encountered as a lament of Jeremiah in chs. 11 f.; 15; 17; 18; 20; and as the lament of the nation in chs. 3:21 to 4:2 and chs. 14:1 to 15:4. The praise of God is found, for example, in chs. 10 and 32. In Isa., chs. 1 to 39, the praise of God is found in the song of the seraphim in ch. 6:3 and at the conclusion of the first book in ch. 12.

The Book of Amos can best show how all three major forms can be present in a small, very compact corpus of a prophetic book:

A. Ch. 7:10-17 is an account and in chs. 7 to 9 are vision accounts.

B. Almost everything else is prophetic speech.

C. The doxologies, chs. 4:13; 5:8-9; 9:5-6, are praise of God.

A lament is intimated in the vision accounts (by a prayer of intercession, cf. Würthwein). In determining the prophetic speech forms one can begin with these three major forms. A and B are more closely related to each other inasmuch as many of the accounts that are contained in the prophetic books include prophetic speeches *in themselves.* Three examples can be cited:

In Amos 7:1-17 the prophetic speech is found in vs. 14-17.

In Isa., chs. 7 and 8, the account contains prophetic speeches, e.g., 7:4-9 and also chs. 36 to 39.

In The Book of Jeremiah a whole layer of tradition, the Baruch narrative, contains speeches of the prophet which are embedded in the account, e.g., the temple speech in Jer., ch. 26 (cf. v. 7).

These three major forms are confirmed as the basic elements of the tradition in the prophetic books in that they represent at the same time — and this is certainly no accident — the basic forms of the three parts of the canon: the account is the basic form of the historical books, and speech to God in the form of lament and praise is the basic form of the Psalter.

The first outlines of the history of the prophetic speech can be derived from these three major forms. In an early period, the time before the writing prophets, the prophetic word was transmitted only in the body of the account. Whether these prophetic narratives and legends in the books of Samuel, Kings, and Chronicles have passed down the genuine prophetic speeches or have altered them can be neither summarily affirmed nor denied here at the beginning. This is to be determined case by case from the viewpoint of the heart of the tradition. In all events the earlier history of the prophetic speech must be taken into consideration.

In the second period — the eighth and seventh centuries — the prophetic speeches as such have become so intensely historical that they are collected and form the matrix of the prophetic books of both of these centuries. During the exile, both major forms, B and C, are brought into relation in the prophecy of Deutero-Isaiah and the prophetic speech is permeated by the prayer form and by motifs from The Psalms. At the same time during the exile, the prophetic speech was united with Priestly speech forms by Ezekiel. From then on, only mixed forms are found until prophecy turns into apocalyptic.

This survey should show that the prophetic speech of the eight and seventh centuries must be seen in the middle between the account and the utterance directed to God. While only a broad outline has been indicated here, a comprehensive description would have to supplement this by pointing out first that cult prophecy, from the beginning,

92

contained strong elements of the service of worship. An example is The Book of Habakkuk, which begins (ch. 1:2-4, 12 f.) and concludes (ch. 3:18) as a Psalm, and exhibits even more Psalm motifs.

In the following study, the actual prophetic speech should be defined according to its forms after setting aside the passages in the form of accounts and utterances directed toward God. To do this one begins with that which a word in the Old Testament really is — a personal event to which speaking as well as hearing belongs; a kind of happening that moves from one person (the one speaking) to another person (the one hearing).[2] Three questions arise from the character of this word: *Who speaks? To whom does he speak? What takes place in this speaking?*

The first question has to do with the origin of the prophetic word. This origin is not unambiguous. It is a word of the prophet, but as such, it claims to be God's word. What is to be made of this claim? How are both of these subjects to be related to one another? The prophetic texts themselves clearly have something to say regarding this question. The sentence found throughout the whole of prophecy by which the prophetic word is authorized as the word of God, " Thus says Yahweh " (or said), is the message formula that is used repeatedly and very widely in profane speech. The prophet, as a messenger of God who delivers God's word, understands himself as the bearer of a message. Hence, behind this first question, Who speaks in the prophetic speech? there are others that must be clarified: What is a messenger-speech? What does it mean that the prophets have understood themselves as messengers of God? To what extent is the prophetic speech to be understood as a messenger's speech? and, Does the prophetic office consist of only service as a messenger?

The second question concerns the person addressed. Two major groups quickly emerge: speeches to Israel and speeches to other nations. The first group falls into the fol-

93

lowing divisions: the speech can be addressed to an individual, to a group, or to the whole nation. The second group does not have such clear subdivisions. The oracles against the foreign nations are almost always directed to the particular nation as a whole.

The third question, What takes place in this speaking? should at first only disclose what is by far the most predominant function of the prophetic speech: An announcement is almost always made in it. That something else can occur in this announcement as well may remain as an open possibility here at the outset. In a way quite similar to the second question, two major groups also emerge at first glance from the third: the announcement can proclaim judgment or salvation.

It is clear that the second question must always be kept in mind with the third. In the judgment as well as the salvation announcement one must always ask to whom it is directed. If one is able to view the prophetic books in the form in which they have been passed down to us from the viewpoint of these three fundamental questions, then one can be certain that all three questions have developed in conjunction with one another.

What the first question concerns is shown by the claim that is underscored and reiterated in the titles of the books and a multitude of redactional additions in all of the prophetic books, that in the words spoken by the prophets one is dealing with the word of God. And indeed, one can see a tendency that clearly augments this: the introductory formulas that identify the speech of the prophet as the word of God are more numerous in the later books, and also in the later period. This is especially true in the books of the Former Prophets where the " word of Yahweh " has been inserted many times.

In view of this massive tendency to identify the speech of the prophet as the word of God, the fact appears still more clearly that the first question concerning the author of the prophetic speech does not permit a division into two

94

groups — (a) the word of God, (b) the word of the prophet — as do the second and third questions. One cannot find even the beginnings of such a division in the prophetic books. Wilderberger's work is able to show, rather, that in The Book of Jeremiah, where such clear criteria for this distinction are present, a literary separation of the word of Yahweh and the word of the prophet is *not* possible. Even in those places where we have subsequently attempted to find such a distinction, the tradition has designated an increasing number of prophetic speeches, which are clearly recognizable as such, as speeches of Yahweh, even where they do not claim to be messengers' speeches (Wildberger indicates that many times).

The second question, concerning the person to whom the prophetic speech is addressed, has coincided in a considerable number of cases with the collection and arrangement of the prophetic speeches. The schema that one finds most frequently in the construction of the prophetic books is the following:

I. Judgment-speeches to the prophet's own nation
II. Judgment-speeches to foreign nations
III. Salvation-speeches to the prophet's own nation
(IV. Accounts)

Collections of oracles against foreign nations are found in Amos, Isaiah, Jeremiah, and Ezekiel. Otherwise, small collections of them are encountered separately, e.g., in the booklet Obadiah. There can thus be no doubt that the person to whom the speech was addressed was considered by those who collected and passed down the prophetic speeches to be an important criterion for determining the types of speeches.

Within the speeches to the nation, however, those who transmitted the books have set particular groups apart. Thus in Jer., chs. 20 to 23, the speeches to the leading people, the kings and the prophets, have been placed together — an indication that those who passed them down considered the person to whom the speeches were addressed as very important for the organization of the whole.

The same holds true for the third question even though here it is not so clearly recognizable. The schema that was given above already shows that. In the books of Jeremiah and Ezekiel collections of salvation-speeches are discernible (Jer., chs. 30 to 33; Ezek., chs. 33 to 39 and 48, respectively). In Isa., chs. 1 to 39, whole collections of salvation-speeches cannot be found, yet here, a salvation-speech has often been joined to the end of a group of judgment-speeches: chs. 2:1-4; 4:2-6; 9:1-6; 11:1-9; similar to Amos 9:8b-15 at the end of the group in chs. 3 to 9. On the whole, one can still recognize that the judgment- and salvation-speeches do not run indiscriminately through one another, but are clearly contrasted to one another. Now we can provisionally establish that the traditionists could not perceive any types of groups other than those of judgment and salvation announcements.

The three questions that we have found to be fundamental to the arrangement and the composition of the specific prophetic speeches are not our questions only. They were already known to those who passed down the prophetic books. Here at the outset, therefore, we have not applied a foreign standard to the prophetic books with these three questions, but stand entirely in the succession of the traditionists.

From these criteria which were obtained from the prophetic books themselves the following groups have emerged so far:

Speeches to Israel — Speeches to Foreign Nations
Announcements of Judgment — Announcements of Salvation

Both criteria must be combined in each case. Always, however, we are dealing with an announcement. We must now raise a question even though it cannot yet be completely answered: Are there still other independent genres besides the announcement? If one begins with the whole prophetic book as it stands in its final form, then it must be stated at the outset that neither exhorting-, nor reproaching-, nor warning-speeches are to be recognized in the collections of the prophetic speeches as a particular form that was acknowledged and utilized by the collectors. Such groupings are not to be found in any of the prophetic books. This division cannot look to the traditionists for support. Certainly that is related to the incongruence between salvation- and judgment-speeches which is so very important for the arrangement of the prophetic books. The announcements of doom or judgment by the prophets are grounded — they include a reason. That does not mean that this must be the case each time without exception; as a whole, however, the reason belongs to the genre of the announcement of judgment and its absence is the exception. The reason is an essential component of the announcement of judgment; for the person addressed, it has the meaning of " making [this] acceptable " (H. W. Wolff). It follows from this that accusation *necessarily* belongs to the announcement of judgment as a reason. This reason can, of course, stand in a loose connection with the announcement of judgment. Occasionally it can become independent as an accusation, since it can be greatly expanded and become separated from the announcement. For all that, however, it is not an independent genre, but is in its origin and nature a component part of the announcement of judgment.

The same thing, however, does not hold true for the announcement of salvation. The announcement of salvation *can* not be grounded in the same way as the announcement of judgment. The reason for this is found in the nature of the relationship between God and man: when God announces salvation to an individual or nation in correspondence with the announcement of judgment, then that is not based upon a positive, deserving deed of man, but upon God's *hesed,* upon his " faithfulness to the covenant," his love, his mercy; in any case, upon God's graceful turning toward his people. Here lies the necessary incongruence

97

between a salvation and judgment announcement; here is the reason that by nature, the announcement of salvation does not have two parts as does the announcement of judgment. (It is from this perspective that Jer. 28:7-9 is to be understood.) Because of this, exhortation and warning, where they are encountered, cannot have the same function as the reason in the announcement of judgment. Likewise, they cannot be simply placed in the same category with it.

One may conclude then that the exhortation and warning are not independent prophetic speech genres, but represent expansions of the original prophetic speech forms. The task remaining now is to further investigate separately the major genres which were derived from the prophetic books themselves. In this investigation we may be led by the three questions that emerged from the structure of the prophetic speech, and at the outset we may turn to the first question: Who speaks? [2a]

II. THE PROPHETIC SPEECH AS THE SPEECH OF A MESSENGER

The presupposition of the understanding of the prophetic speech as a messenger's speech is that from the viewpoint of the Bible as a whole God is not bound to this form of revelation, that there have been other modes of revelation before and after prophecy, and that prophecy, therefore, belongs to a definite period of time and is bound to this period.

It is the period of time from the formation of the state to the loss of statehood in Israel — thus, almost exactly the time of the kingdoms.[3] Prophecy for Israel has, therefore, a temporally limited rather than an all-embracing significance. Generalizations must be avoided. If the epoch of

98

prophecy coincides with the epoch of the kingdom in Israel, then this cannot fail to have some significance for the particular form of the revelation which comes in the speech of the messenger. It presupposes at the same time a higher guiding authority whose claim to guide the nation in ways that were willed, initiated, and directed by God were not disputed. The same holds true for cultic guidance which was tied in very closely with the kingdom and which was given by the priests in the temples. The prophets, thus, never demanded that the word of God that came forth through them — the messenger's word — would have to take the place of the word that was cultically mediated. In all of the sharp criticism of the kingdom as well as of the priesthood, cult prophecy, and temples, no prophetic speeches have been passed down to us that demanded a total change in the political or cultic spheres.[4] Prophecy, therefore, does not have a revolutionary character in either one of these areas.[5]

It had to sound a call in a certain hour. The prophetic speech as a messenger's speech is not then a form of revelation that is valid everywhere and for all times, but is one that would have been considered necessary for this period of time, within these limits.

Perhaps it is possible to determine theologically the time of prophecy more closely. Such an attempt, however, may only be made with great caution.

The revelation of God *before* the prophetic era is characterized by directness. In the patriarchal stories God speaks directly to Abraham, Isaac, and Jacob. In the primeval history it is true as well — God speaks to Adam and Eve, to Cain and to Noah. The direct speech of God to Moses is also a strand that runs throughout the Mosaic tradition. A transition is seen in the Joseph story where God reveals himself through a dream. At no time does God speak directly to Joseph. Another transition form that is found during the period between the Patriarchs and the Judges is that of the *mal'āk yhwh,* the messenger of God.

He is a different type of messenger from the prophet insofar as the *mal'āk yhwh* exists only during his message and not as a person who continues to exist; yet, one can see a clear connection to the prophets in that he also announces something (mostly salvation). In any case, the *mal'āk yhwh* is a transitional mode of appearance between the directness of God's revelation and his withdrawal into the distance. *After* the epoch of prophecy, one can see a tendency to make God more transcendent. This is recognizable in many places and is generally acknowledged by those who have investigated this problem. After the end of prophecy, the direct as well as the indirect revelation of God belongs to the past — the word of God is now identical with the existent written word. So, prophecy is to be defined as a transitional stage in which the speech of the messenger is the form designated for the indirect revelation of God. God speaks no longer to the king,[6] no longer directly in signs, or from the lot-casting oracle,[7] and no longer by passing sentence upon the whole nation; God sends messengers.

The Sending of the Messenger

A multitude of examples of the formula " Thus spoke NN " have been handed down as a part of a message both in the Old Testament and elsewhere. The formula authorizes the message, which is repeated by the messenger before the addressee, to be the word of the sender, corresponding, therefore, to the signature in our letter form.

The " messenger formula " stems from the time before the invention of writing — from the time, therefore, in which the transmission of a speech to a place faraway was confined to the messengers' oral repetition alone — from a time, thus, when the oral message had a meaning no longer conceivable to us today.

The example of how a messenger was sent, referred to by Köhler, is in the patriarchal stories, Gen. 32:3-5:

Report of the sending:	And Jacob sent messengers before him
Addressee:	to Esau his brother
Place:	in the land of Seir, the country of Edom,
Introduction to the commissioning:	instructing them,
Commissioning of the messenger:	"Thus you shall say to my lord Esau;
Messenger formula:	Thus says your servant Jacob,
Messenger's speech: reporting section:	'I have sojourned with Laban, and stayed until now; and I have oxen, asses, flocks, menservants, and maidservants;
final section:	and I have sent to tell my lord, in order that I may find favor in your sight.'"

Since the messenger formula is found in the middle of this example, it can clearly illustrate its function. The message consists of three events: (1) commissioning, (2) transmission, (3) delivery. The most important of these three events is the second, the transmission. It is expressed in the introductory report, which contains in the verb "to send" the commission to go to the addressee and the designated place. Before the transmission comes the act of commissioning, consisting of, (a) instruction to the messenger, (b) messenger formula, (c) messenger's speech. The third event is not reported as such in most of the narratives about the sending of a messenger, because it simply contains the execution of the instruction. It consists of the repetition before the addressee of the messenger's speech (i.e., of the transmission of the speech) at the place to which the messenger was sent. Now the messenger again begins his repe-

101

tition of the message with the messenger formula. In the process of sending a message, then, the messenger formula has a twofold place; it occurs two times: the sender first introduces his speech with it — that means that in the presence of the messenger whom he sends he authorizes the speech that is introduced with this formula as *his* speech; then when the messenger has arrived, he introduces the message that has been entrusted to him with the formula, and in this way authorizes it as the speech of the person who had sent him. Because of these two places in which the messenger formula occurs, the Hebrew perfect *'āmar* cannot be clearly rendered by our present or perfect tense. If we are thinking of the moment of the commissioning, then we must say, " Thus says NN "; but if we are thinking of the moment of the delivery, then it is more exact to say, " Thus said NN."

It may be assumed that, along with the messenger formula in the prophetic speech, the whole message-sending procedure was carried over into the occurrence of prophecy. So, not only the origin of the messenger formula is shown here, but we have as well gained access to the structure of the event that we call prophecy. The three stages that constituted a message can be assumed also for the sending of a prophet: (1) the commissioning, (2) the transmission, (3) the delivery.

Indeed, the prophetic tradition exhibits the elements of the message-transmission procedure with astonishing clarity throughout its entire history. The prophets have designated themselves as messengers of God and were understood as such by those to whom they brought their messages. Prophecy must then be understood from the viewpoint of the message-transmission procedure. Though that has already been said in a number of more recent works,[8] this probably has more consequences than have yet been seen. One consequence can easily be indicated here. We said that the most important stage in the sending of a message is the middle one, the transmission. It is in the act of bridging the dis-

102

tance that it has its distinctive meaning. That must have been true also of the prophets. This distance is the basic reason that God sends the messenger. The real problem of the prophets is to bridge this distance with each of their speeches. That those who transmitted the prophetic speeches were conscious of this as the real task of the prophetic speech is seen in the formulation of the commissioning, which is almost always: " Go and say. . .! " (See below.) *Each time* the prophet has to bridge this distance *anew* with his word.

One can say that the " ecstatic theory " isolated and emphasized the *first* part of this event — the " reception of the word." The present phase of the prophetic investigation places too much importance on the *third* part — the delivery of the word — and isolates it too much. The middle part of this event — the bridging of the distance — is not sufficiently valued by either of these explanations. It is, however, only from this middle part that the reception and delivery of the speeches by the prophets is given its meaning. We will have to pay particularly close attention to this structure in seeking to define and understand prophecy.

In antiquity the message procedure and style have a great significance. They are the same for the whole ancient Orient over a very long period of time. Here reference can be made to the works of L. Köhler, J. Lindblom, G. Widengren, Otto Schröder, A. Ungnad, and E. Ebeling which show examples of this. Above all, it is important for prophecy that these examples show the most frequently encountered introductory formula in the ancient Babylonian letters to be: " To Y say: so (says) X . . ." (or similar) which was actually the formula for the *oral* message transmission that was taken over into the letter style (Widengren perceived this as well, *op. cit.,* p. 61: " It is thus presupposed that the letter is only the literary fixation of an oral message which is brought to the addressee by a messenger. The formula shows that there is a close connection between the oral

103

message and the written letter "). That is indirectly confirmed by Lindblom's statement that this introductory formula first began to recede noticeably in the Neo-Assyrian and Neo-Babylonian times. One can see that the oral procedure for sending a message still lives in these formulas centuries after the first technicalization of the message through writing was accomplished. This fact shows the high significance that the commissioning of a messenger and the messenger formula had at one time. Something of the character of the oral message was still retained as well in the transmission of a written message as seen in an example offered by Widengren (*op. cit.*, p. 60). In a Parthian text the transmission of a letter is described as follows:

> And they entered and presented homage onto King Vistasp
> and handed over the letter.
> Awraham, the chief of the scribes, rose on his feet
> and read the letter in a loud voice.

In relation to this he refers to II Kings 18:28, where the field commander Rabshakeh delivers a message from the great king to the people of Jerusalem:

> Hear the word of the great king, the king of Assyria!
> Thus says the king:
> " Do not let Hezekiah deceive you, for he will not be able
> to deliver you out of my hand."

That is important for the use of the message style in prophecy insofar as it is the *oral* transmission alone which is possible here. Hearing belongs to the character of the reception of the message as well as to the repetition of the speech, i.e., to the delivery of the message. The whole phenomenon of prophecy was not possible at just any time in world history, but only in this epoch in which the oral message was still a message in a real sense. The appropriation of the message style, therefore, shows from another viewpoint, how prophecy was bound to the times. That can be shown in another related example: The concept of " verbal

104

inspiration " that came into use in Judaism and passed over into the Christian church could only arise in an epoch in which the word no longer had validity in an oral form, but rather, had to be written.

One can understand how the invention of writing and the feasibility of having written messages which followed from it, permitted that which was the most important for the oral message to recede into the background, i.e., the bringing of words over a distance by a living man upon whose dependable retention of and repetition of the words *alone* rested the possibility of sending a message. The sending of a message was preeminently a personal event. It is in the light of this high significance given to the messenger in the time of the oral message that prophecy is to be understood. When again and again in recent times the prophet has been called " the mouthpiece of God," it is a sign of a deep misunderstanding of prophecy! At no time can a messenger become a mouthpiece.

It follows from the requirements of the oral transmission that the message that the messenger has to deliver must be short. Some wanted to draw the same conclusion from the ecstatic character of prophecy (Gunkel, Hölscher). The shortness of a few sounds that are ejaculated in ecstasy (evidenced only extremely seldom in the prophecy which has been transmitted to us) is something essentially different from the brevity of a message that must be exact and suitable for retention immediately. Above all, it must be understandable. A message that is *only* received and repeated orally must strive to be both understandable and retainable since there are always just brief moments in which the message is learned — a few moments upon which *everything* related to the message depends. If this is correct, then Gunkel's description of the prophetic style, which many exegetes have followed, must be fundamentally revised. This characterization proves to be correct for a few of the prophetic speeches but not for the majority. The dark, disconnected, hurried, and desultory style is *not* to be found

105

in the vast majority of the prophetic speeches, but rather, their style is much more pronouncedly bright, understandable, and decided.

As far as the brevity is concerned, it, too, is not so simple as this. Just a survey can show that the very short speech stands in the beginning of the history of prophecy, the relatively short speech continues to be predominant in the prophecy of the eighth and seventh centuries, and then from Ezekiel on, the prophetic speech becomes very long.

Other than the message situation, can the messenger-commissioning that is recounted in the Old Testament produce anything else comparable with regard to the messenger's speech? Can one observe common features in the historical books which might be of significance for the prophetic speech?

Again, we will begin with a passage from the patriarchal stories. Joseph sends a message to his father from Egypt (Gen. 45:9) :

> Make haste and go up to my father and say to him,
> " Thus says your son Joseph,
> God has made me lord of all Egypt;
> come down to me, do not tarry."

The first sentence contains the commissioning of a messenger, and that is in the form of a double commission: Go and say! The second sentence is the messenger formula which is given a special importance by the context (will the father believe it?) . The message that now follows clearly consists of two parts; it contains a report (perfect) and a summons (imperative) . The meaning and connection of both parts of the message is completely clear. The first part is simply a report in which he describes the situation, and is indeed extremely short, containing only what is necessary for the receiver of the message to know. This account aims only at giving a basis for the imperative part of the message; Jacob can risk coming after his son since Joseph

106

has become something in the meantime. The message, therefore, in all its brevity has two parts. The tendency of one part of the message (perfect) is to serve as a reason for the other (imperative). The imperative section contains the intention of the message that Joseph sends to his father; he wants to come and get his father. In order to enable the father to accept this invitation and follow through with it, he joins to it the section giving the reason. The message of Hezekiah to Isaiah in II Kings 19:2-4 has the same structure; see also Num. 20:14-17.

Another example is offered by the Balaam story; here as well, the sender of the message invites the addressee to come to him:

> Num. 22:5 f.: (and he) sent messengers to Balaam . . . ,
> saying,
> "Behold, a people has come out of Egypt;
> . . . and they are dwelling. . . .
> Come now, curse this people."
> 15 ff.: Once again Balak sent princes. . . .
> And they came to Balaam and said to him,
> "Thus says Balak the son of Zippor:
> 'Let nothing hinder you from coming to me;
> for I will surely do you great honor, and . . .' "

The agreement between the first message to Balaam and the message in Gen. 45:9 is clear at the first glance. The differences are the result of the different situations. The commissioning of the messenger and messenger formula are both abbreviated here; *lē' mōr* simply stands for both. This follows from the formulation of the second message where the messenger commissioning and messenger formula are complete, but with the variation that not the commissioning but the execution of the commission is described. This is a beautiful example for showing the possibilities for varying the description of a message procedure.

In regard to content the imperative part of the second message is the same; only the formulation is different. But the reason, on the other hand, is essentially different here.

107

In the first message the commission to Balaam was based simply upon the situation into which he was called; that corresponds exactly to the relation of the perfect and the imperative parts of Gen. 45:9. In the second message, however, the request for Balaam to come is reinforced in that Balak gives him the prospect of a high reward. Yet, this part of the message which pertains to the future has the same function as the perfect part in the foregoing; it should reinforce the summons for Balaam to come.

The same basic elements should be recognized again in the message of the king of Assyria to Hezekiah and the people of Jerusalem delivered by his field commander in II Kings 18:19-35. A section of the message is in the perfect tense; the hopeless plight of Jerusalem laid waste by Assyria, as it was seen from Assyria's viewpoint. This is followed by a section in the imperfect: the command to capitulate (addressed indirectly to the king and directly to the people). As in the second message of Balak to Balaam the people of Jerusalem are presented a picture of their good prospects in the event of their capitulation. On the other hand, this message in II Kings 18:19-35 is basically different from the messages mentioned previously by virtue of its length; this is no longer a message that is literally repeated, but one that is elaborated. The reason for this is clearly recognizable; the one who transmits the message of the king is not only a messenger but also a field commander. As such he has the full authority to speak the message in his own words from his situation as field commander, e.g., this is seen in the division of the elements of the message so that they are directed to the king and the people — a division that certainly grows out of the situation. In regard to the elements of the message of the king, the commander has changed nothing; the perfect as well as the imperfect parts of the message that the king had imparted to his commander could nevertheless have been *very* short. Inasmuch as the long message only elaborates both of these parts, the commander has not altered the message that the
108

king imparted to him. This example will be especially important for the transmission of the prophetic message; the first glance over the difference, particularly the quite different length of the prophets' speeches, shows that here also, the literally transmitted message and the elaborated message have existed alongside each other.

In regard to the third element of the message it might be further pointed out that in the second message to the people something like a (conditional) promise is added to the imperative part:

Make your peace with me and come out to me; then every one of you will eat of his own vine, and every one of his own fig tree.

It is the same placing-in-prospect of salvation that was intended to reinforce the request in Balak's message for Balaam to come. The " conditional announcement of salvation " is a form that is frequently used in the later prophecy. It will not be of minor importance that this form occurred fairly often in the messages.

Lindblom accepts another different root for the messenger formula: " The oracle formula, ' thus says the Lord,' goes back on the one hand to the proclamation formula of the ancient Oriental declarations and decrees, and on the other hand to the formula with which the message used to be introduced " (p. 102).

It is questionable to me whether a different root of the messenger formula is actually shown here. Lindblom cites the Edict of Cyrus in II Chron. 36:22 ff. and Ezra 1:1-4 as the first example of such a royal decree. This royal decree namely shows exactly the same structure as the messages in Gen., ch. 45, and Num., ch. 22. It consists of a perfect and an imperative part:

II Chron. 36:23:
Thus says Cyrus king of Persia, " The Lord, the God of heaven, has given me all the kingdoms of the earth, and he has charged me to build him a house at Jerusalem, which is

109

in Judah. Whoever is among you of all his people, may the Lord his God be with him. Let him go up."

The distinction lies in the situation: Here the message of a king is issued and it goes out to a great circle of men. As a decree of the king, however, it is a true message though it has a special form. The relation of both parts to each other is the same as in Joseph's message to Jacob. The real purpose of the message is the decree — the release and return of the Jews, and the building of the Temple in Jerusalem. The king, however, adds the presuppositions upon which it is formed — the power that has been given to him as lord of the world and the divine commission that he had received.

Besides this there is the mere transmission of a command, I Kings 20:3; 2:30; II Kings 1:9, 11, or the transmission of a question, II Kings 1:2. It seems to me that something different from a message in the proper sense is present here; perhaps only the extension of a command or a question by the transmitter. The distinction can best be shown in I Kings 2:30. Joab has taken refuge in the Temple and Benaiah comes to meet him with the words: " The king commands, ' Come forth.' " The sense here is not that the king wants to transmit a message to Joab through Benaiah, but rather, that the king has commanded the arrest of Joab, and Benaiah executes the arrest in the name of the king. Or, when Benhadad of Syria sends the following word to Ahab:

Thus says Benhadad:
" Your silver and your gold are mine;
your fairest wives and children also are mine."

This corresponds somewhat to what we call an ultimatum. The ultimatum does not intend to influence the addressee in order to move him toward a decision as does the two-part message, but compels him in the same way that an authoritative command compels one. These speeches are also formed in the manner of a message (ch. 20:2: " He sent

110

messengers into the city to Ahab "), but a message of an essentially different type than the other group of two-part messages.

To that extent Lindblom's distinction between a message formula and a proclamation formula is justified, but in a somewhat different way than he saw. The proclamation formula introduces royal decrees, ordinances, and commands inasmuch as these convey irrevocable authoritative words of the king; the message formula introduces the message consisting of a perfect and an imperative part, which still offers a decision to the addressee.

There can still be many other possible types of messages. The passages that have been investigated here, however (Lindblom has cited most of these in his investigation), show not only that the message formula affects the framework of the message by giving it a fixed form but that a fixed form can even be seen in the messages (messenger-speeches) themselves. Obviously, any ordinary speech cannot be made into a message by inserting it into the framework of a messenger's speech, thus prefacing it with the aforementioned formula; *the speech itself which is to be transmitted assumes, as a message, definite, fixed forms which first make it into a message.*

This observation which has been made of the profane messenger-speech is of great significance in respect to the prophetic speech as the speech of a messenger. Not every ordinary speech that is prefaced by " thus says the Lord " (or the like) turns out to be a messenger's speech; rather, it can be assumed from the outset that the prophetic speech as the speech of a messenger has definite and evident forms that make it into a messenger's speech.

It follows from this that:

1. *All* prophetic speech forms are to be examined first of all as to whether they are and intend to be messages and how they are to be understood as messages.
2. It must be asked whether the two-part message corresponds to the prophetic speech.

111

3. One must ask whether and how a speech whose very nature requires directness (as the reproaching-speech) is altered in order to become a message.

In addition to this, a characteristic type of message might be pointed out: a negotiation carried out through messengers which is an early semblance of what we call a diplomatic negotiation. The best example is in Judg. 11:12 ff.:

12:	Then Jephthah sent messengers to the king of the Ammonites and said,
(Accusation in perfect)	"What have you against me, that you have come to me to fight against my land?"
13:	And the king of the Ammonites answered the messengers of Jephthah,
(Reason in imperative)	"Because Israel on coming from Egypt took away my land, from the . . . ; now therefore restore it peaceably."
14:	And Jephthah sent messengers again to the king of the Ammonites
15:	and said to him, "Thus says Jephthah:
(Dispute)	Israel did not take away the land of Moab or the land of the Ammonites,
16-20: (Explanation)	but when they came up from Egypt.
	. . .
27: (Dispute)	I therefore have not sinned against you,
(Accusation)	and you do me wrong by making war on me;
(Appeal to a higher court)	the Lord, the Judge, decide this day between the people of Israel and the people of Ammon."
28:	But the king of the Ammonites did not heed the message of Jephthah which he sent to him.
29:	Then the Spirit of the Lord came upon Jephthah.

Here a regular negotiation is described which was carried out by messengers. The first message of Jephthah begins with the fact of the warlike invasion by the Ammonite king and seeks to know the legal grounds for it. The answer of the Ammonite king has two parts: A perfect part states the reason that has moved him (allegedly) to attack Israel, and an imperative part is attached demanding Israel's territory east of the Jordan. To this a promise is added: if Israel will relinquish this territory, he will peacefully withdraw. Then Jephthah sends another message. This message also has two parts. The perfect part consists of an argument against the reason which the Ammonite king had given for his invasion. This reason (vs. 16-20) is so broad that it is no longer a simple message but an explanatory elaboration, and is itself a piece of historical description which has grown out of an altercation with a neighboring nation. In place of the imperative part comes something completely different — an announcement. The matter is not to be settled through diplomatic negotiation, for assertion stands against assertion; a higher authority must therefore decide, i.e., God. Practically speaking, the sentence means that the weapons must now decide!

The account of this decision begins by saying immediately that the spirit of Yahweh came over Jephthah, i.e., the impulse toward a Yahweh-war was given; after this it says (v. 32), " and the Lord gave them into his hand."

The whole appears to be a legal negotiation between two widely separated parties that must therefore be carried on by means of messengers It was caused by a misdeed of A (Ammon) against I (Israel). The occasion of the first message is therefore a misdeed done by the addressee of this message. (Formally, this is exactly the same as the messages that God sends to Israel by the prophets; they are occasioned by a misdeed of Israel.) It inquires about the legal grounds of the inimical act. Naturally the message is not meant to be an inquiry only, but rather, has the character of a remonstrance, or an indirect accusation, since it presupposes that the opponent has *no* sufficient reason for his misdeed. It intends to say: We have done nothing to you! So why have you done this . . . ?

One such accusing question is found in the prophetic

113

speeches in a way that is formally similar, e.g., Jer. 2:5, "What wrong did your fathers find in me that they . . . ?"

Apart from this similarity, however, Jephthah's first message shows the situation in which an accusing question or a remonstrating question can become a part of a message: when a misdeed is under discussion and the one to whom it happened asks the distant party through a messenger about the legal grounds for his action.

If one examines just the message of A alone, it proves to be a typical message with a perfect and imperfect part (the promise is connected to this) . The possibility must be considered that this message, as a historical fact, came to be fundamental to the whole story and that the negotiation that surrounds it was told only as the description of the altercation between Ammon and Israel in that period.

If one can gather this negotiation together into one event by reducing it to its results, then the remaining content of Jephthah's message is: You have no reason for attacking us and your invasion is a transgression. Now the arms will speak (cf. in the prophetic speech: Reason and Announcement). The type of the two-part message is again in evidence in this negotiation through a messenger, but in different forms.

The accounts of the commissioning of a messenger which are dealt with here only represent a mere segment; they have had such a significance in the ancient world that a more intensive study is required which does not limit itself to the Old Testament. Although there are many possibilities for messages, the few examples that were dealt with here have already shown that there are *types of messages.* It is thus probable that mere news (of an event) is to be distinguished from a message. Among the messages there is a type that places the entire stress on the perfect part (is it the same as news?) , and a type in which the meaning of the message comes in the imperative part. Besides these there is the transmission of commands and questions, of an inquiry through a messenger, a warning, a reminder, state-

114

ments of cooperation, etc. Messages in the various realms of life are to be distinguished, such as the personal, the political, and above all, court life. All of this deserves a comprehensive investigation that cannot be made here. A further question must be raised: Is the herald's call (or the proclamation by a herald) a form that is independent of the message or only a variation of the usual message?

The Message of God and the Sending of a Messenger (the Mari Letters)

The sending of messages and messengers by God or a god can occur not only in prophecy but in other ancient religions as well. In the Old Testament there are *mal'āk yhwh* — angels of God before and at the same time as the prophets. In many religions there is an abundance of parallels to the " angels " as messengers of the gods. In polytheism the messenger of the gods (Hermes) is himself a god, or the messengers are divine creatures; in any case they belong on the side of the gods.[9]

The possibility of a man's being able to deliver the message of God to other men is something essentially different. Actually there is something about this that is absurd and impossible to the ancient world; a messenger of God can actually only be a god or a divine creature! To designate a man as a messenger of God is thus hardly possible. In Isa. 6:8 it does not say that; here it reads, " Whom shall I send, and who will go for us? " The messenger service here is therefore consciously circumlocutory because a man cannot be designated as the messenger of God. It is thus not accidental that this first became possible at the end of prophecy:

Mal. 3:1: " Behold, I send my messenger to prepare the way before me."

This is the reason that no very specific name is given in the Old Testament for the writing prophets. In their com-

115

missioning, as it is most clearly described in Isa., ch. 6, they come close to being designated as messengers of God. That did not happen for the reason just given. They were thus called by the broader name, *nābî'*, even if that led to mis-understandings. However a *nābî'* is to be understood — it is, in any case, not the specific name of the judgment prophets of the eighth and seventh centuries. Even if we might know what the contemporaries of Amos and Isaiah understood by the word *nābî'*, we would still not know what kind of commission these men had. It is entirely understandable, however, that the disciples of Jesus were given the name *apostoloi* by the early community. They were not exactly messengers of God, but the messengers of one who had sent them forth while standing next to them on this earth and speaking in their language. This glance at the *apostoloi* of the New Testament shows something more. A necessary aspect of " messengerhood " (*Bote-Sein*) is the sending of one who, himself, is *not* an envoy, but is something essentially different. The apostles did not call their students to be apostles as well; the apostles are called only for special times. Neither the " disciples " of Isaiah, nor Baruch, the disciple of Jeremiah, followed their masters as prophets. They were not sent.

It is thus understandable that there is no explicit, institutionally defined office of messenger of God in any of the religions known to us. Certainly, there are divine, or half-divine messengers of the gods in many religions; on the other side there is the seer, the mantic, and the oracle priest as a continuing office, but not the messenger of God. It is also certainly characteristic of Israel that even though there was a series of such messengers of God which followed one another, and in some cases worked at the same time, a continuing institution or a prophetic office did not develop. It was completely justified when the Israelitic phenomenon of prophecy was explained in almost all of the previous investigations as something unique in the history of religions.

Now this " unique " must be carefully limited, due to

116

the discovery of the Mari letters in which the delivery of a message of a god through a man is reported. After their editing of these texts,[10] W. von Soden, M. Noth, H. W. Wolff, H. Schmökel, and others considered their meaning for prophecy. They all agree that formally this represents a genuine parallel and even more that an indirect historical connection is possible, or at least is not yet excluded. In regard to their content, however, the individual character of Old Testament prophecy appears even more clearly against the background of this formal parallel. M. Noth says (op. cit., p. 239):

" These agreements are not likely to be accidental, and are all the less likely to be so since nothing other than this has yet been found in the whole of the ancient Orient which is actually comparable. Accordingly, it can hardly be doubted, . . . that in this messenger of God, we are dealing not only with a figure parallel to Old Testament prophecy, but one that belongs to the earlier history of prophecy. . . .

" But just when a historical relation can be assumed, the great distinction between the two forms also becomes immediately obvious. It does not lie in the kind of appearance, but in the content of that which was announced as the message of God. In Mari, the concern is with . . . cultic and political affairs of a quite limited and ephemeral significance."

About the same thing is said by H. W. Wolff and H. Schmökel (op. cit.). W. von Soden presents three points of contiguity (op. cit., p. 402): (1) the god in Mari also demands the repetition of his commands to the king without regard to whether they are agreeable to the king; (2) in Mari, as in the Old Testament, the prophetic speech makes a critique of the behavior of the king; (3) the first letter ends in a salvation prophecy; it is qualified, however, since the presupposition of its occurrence is the fulfillment of the will of God by the king. " On the other hand, the distinctions are clear enough; . . . what is

117

found here does not go beyond the scope of the cult prophecy which was condemned in the Old Testament."

A basically different estimation of the material significance of the Mari texts for Old Testament prophecy is unlikely. But this does not bring its actual significance to light with enough clarity; it lies in the linguistic structure of these texts and they have not yet been adequately analyzed and described in comparison with the speech forms of Old Testament prophecy. Below, I have summarized the preliminary results of such an investigation:

1. *The Reception of Revelation.* As W. von Soden (and others) has seen, the Mari texts deal with cult prophecy. In making a comparison with the Old Testament the first question to be raised is whether these texts produce criteria that would enable a more exact definition of cult prophecy in the Old Testament to be made. In the first letter it is clear and unambiguous that the reception of the revelation is described within the framework of a cultic action (text from W. von Soden) :

> In my dream I and a man with me
> wanted to go from the district of Sagaratum in the upper region to Mari.
> In my vision I went toward Terqa and immediately after my arrival entered the temple of Dagan and cast myself down before Dagan.
> While I was kneeling,
> Dagan opened his mouth and spoke the following to me . . .

The remark at the conclusion of the letter is to be connected with this beginning:

> The man who told me this dream,
> will offer an animal as a sacrifice before Dagan,
> hence I have not sent him . . .

The reception of the word takes place, therefore, in the middle between the prostration before the god and the of-
118

fering of a sacrifice. Word-reception as an event in the cult cannot be described more clearly! It can be established, on the other hand, that such an event as

Prostration before God
Hearing the message of God
Offering of a sacrifice

has no parallel in the prophetic text of the Old Testament. The closest parallel to it is Isa., ch. 6. It is possible that a similar description — even if only remotely similar — is at the basis of this account of Isaiah's call in ch. 6. It is therefore possible that this type of account of a prophet's call may have originated in cult prophecy. Even then, however, it is all the clearer where Isa., ch. 6, diverges from the event described in the first Mari letter. In Isa., ch. 6, the cultic act that was stated at the beginning and the end *is missing;* the prostration in Isa., ch. 6, first comes as a reaction to the appearance of God who is enthroned in his temple, and the sacrificial act is completely transformed into an action of God in relation to Isaiah. Isaiah, ch. 6, then, attests to the way the prophetic vocation emerged out of cult prophecy. (If a cultic background is to be generally accepted for Isa., ch. 6, it thus seems to me that this is more clearly shown by the first Mari letter than by the connection with the kingship ideology as I. Engnell [*The Call of Isaiah,* Uppsala, 1949] attempted to show it.)

Now, however, the event that was just described in the first Mari letter is worded as a dream:

In my dream I and a man with me wanted . . .
In my vision I went toward Terqa . . .

And in conclusion it says,

This man saw this in his dream . . .
The man who told me this dream . . .

In the account both manners of revelation stand side by side, though noticeably unlike, giving one the impression that these were two originally independent kinds of word-

119

reception. That would correspond to the existence of both of these kinds of word-reception at the same time in Israel during the time of the writing prophets, as O. Grether ("Name und Wort Gottes im AT," *BZAW*, 1934) depicted it in his fourth chapter, particularly p. 87:

"One can therefore consider as characteristic of the prophetic period before the great writing prophets, the situation that is observable everywhere in which *dābār*, vision, dream, night vision, and mechanical oracle stand next to one another, the first of these gradually becoming predominant."

2. *The Message of God.* (a) The speech which the god Dagan, gives to the Malik-Dagan, has two parts. The first part is a grievance of the god and the second contains the order which the Malik-Dagan should deliver to the king Zimrilim. It contains a command of god to the king corresponding to the grievance over negligence. The link between these two parts is formed by the words:

Now go! I have sent you.
You will speak to Zimrilim in the following way . . .

In this speech the style of the commissioning of the messenger is exactly parallel to that in Old Testament prophecy. The first and the third sentences together correspond literally to the double commission, "Go, and say . . . ," which appears very often (e.g., Isa. 6:9; Jer. 1:7). The sentence in between, "I have sent you," which is encountered in the second and fourth letters as well, has the same function and the same place as the messenger formula in the Old Testament, "thus spoke Yahweh." So too, this identifies the speech that was spoken by the messenger as that of god who had sent him. Exactly the same sentence is found in Jer. 26:12 and 15, where Jeremiah must prove that his speech has come from God (cf. Noth, *op. cit.*, pp. 238 f.). The accounts of prophetic calls correspond to this in meaning.

120

These sentences which identify the word of god stand between the two parts of the first Mari letter, *after* the sentences that contain a remonstrance against the king (corresponding to the prophetic accusation in the Old Testament), and *before* the sentences that contain the actual message of god (here the command of god to the king is combined with an announcement; in the Old Testament this corresponds to an announcement). Thus in the first Mari letter there is an important confirmation of our observation that the original place of the messenger formula in a two-part message is *in the middle* between both of the parts, after the accusation and before the real message of God.

(b) Both parts of the speech contain a qualified announcement of salvation, the second, direct, and the first, indirect. After the commissioning just cited comes the following speech:

Send your emissaries to me and bring back a complete report to me.
Then I will make the chiefs of the Benjaminites wriggle in a fisherman's basket and put them down before you!

The remonstrance in the first part of the speech corresponds here to the commission, which is connected with an indirect announcement of salvation:

Why does the emissary of Zimrilim not stay in my presence constantly?
And why has he not brought a complete report (over everything) back to me?
If he had, I would already have given the chiefs of the Benjaminites into the hand of Zimrilim many days ago.

In both parts of the speech, therefore, the god offers the prospect of his helpful intervention on behalf of the king under the conditions mentioned. Thus, this kind of prophecy clearly proves to be salvation prophecy which stands in a more or less direct relation to the court of the king. Hence Noth (*op. cit.,* p. 240) has correctly indicated that

121

the appearances of the prophet Gad in II Sam., ch. 24, and Nathan in II Sam., ch. 7, are the closest parallels to this in the Old Testament. Salvation prophecy appears also in the fifth letter, though here the (conditional!) announcement of judgment stands at the beginning in the foreground; the ultimate intention of this speech is also salvation for the king:

> If it is not so and he wants to give me that for which I have wished,
> then, I will give him throne upon throne, house upon house, ground upon ground, city upon city.
> I will also give him the land from the rising to the setting sun.

And in another short message at the end of this letter:

> I, myself, will give to you the land from the rising to the setting sun.

On two points the connection with the salvation prophecy of the Old Testament can still be more precisely shown, even in regard to the speech forms. In the first part of the speech of Dagan the intervention of god appears in the form which is encountered very frequently in the Old Testament in connection with the " holy war "[11]: " I would have . . . given the chiefs of the Benjaminites into the hand of Zimrilim." That this " handing over formula " is not unique to Israel has already been suspected, but the important thing here is the connection with salvation prophecy. In the second part the promise of the god is given in a metaphor that serves to strengthen and underscore the announcement (see above, " make . . . wriggle in a fisherman's basket "). This kind of graphic and at the same time intensified speaking in the announcement of the assisting intervention of god is reminiscent of the promises of political success given by the court prophets in Israel. A special instance of this is in I Kings 22:11, where Zedekiah, the salvation prophet, makes iron horns for himself and says:

122

With these you shall push the Syrians
until they are destroyed.

In Jer., ch. 28, Hananiah's breaking of the yoke that Jeremiah wore is also similar. However, a quite obvious parallel to this is found in Isa. 37:29:

Because you (Sennacherib) . . .
I will put my hook in your nose
    and my bit in your mouth,
and I will turn you back on the way
    by which you came.

Because this correspondence is so clear, it may be considered as certain that the prophecy encountered in the Mari letters corresponds to the salvation prophecy of the Old Testament, and that a historical connection between them is possible.

(c) In all five letters this salvation prophecy is directed to the king. They not only show (primarily the first letter) the close connection of this prophecy with the court and the office of Kingship, but even more the interest of the king himself in these prophetic speeches, *even though* they contain warnings and remonstrances against him. This agrees with the report in I Kings, ch. 22, and with the prophecy of Gad and of Nathan, all of which took place in the court of the king. Corresponding to this is the even more important fact that the prophetic speeches in the Old Testament, which came from the time *before* written prophecy, were always speeches to an individual person and that this person was almost always the king. It can be considered certain, then, that there was a form of prophecy in early Israel — completely corresponding to the Mari letters — which was addressed only to the king.

(d) The relation of this prophecy to the cult is seen in the first letter where the prophet's reception of the message is clearly set in a cultic act. In the other letters, the demand which the prophet gives to the king in the name of the god is an explicit cultic demand. In the second letter the message of the god says:

> God has sent me
> Hurry, write to the king
>> that one may celebrate a sacrifice to the spirit of Jahdullim.

In the fourth letter one finds the following which corresponds to this perfectly:

> Write to your lord,
>> that on the fourteenth day of the coming month
>> an animal sacrifice (?) . . . cult should be carried out.
> Under no condition should one allow the same . . . cult to be neglected.

In the fifth letter:

> Les (animaux) mâles et les vaches livre! (Dossin)

The demands of the gods, respective to the neglect of the king in the first and third letters, are completely different. In the first letter, the god complained over not being instructed about the state of the war, and in the second part of the same letter constant instruction is demanded. The aim of this demand was obviously to secure information about the political events for the god — and perhaps that also means the priesthood of this god — so that he might participate in them. If this demand is made by the salvation prophets, then this may be an indication of the political role played by this type of prophecy. One thinks of the early prophetic narratives in the books of Kings, and of the prophet Nathan, and may also ask whether one of the last surviving examples of this function can still be recognized in Isa., chs. 7 and 8. On the other hand, an entirely different demand of god can be seen in the third letter:

> Do you not (now) want to build that city gate (at all)?
> When will the work be done?
> You have obtained (nothing)!

124

The speech clearly corresponds to the remonstrating question of the first letter, " Why have you not brought back . . . a report? " One speaking in the name of the god urges on the building of an edifice that is necessary for the community by reproaching the negligent. Here, the characteristics of this speech are quite similar to the prophecy of Haggai (and Zechariah) ! This parallel enables one to conclude safely that the prophets who urged on the building of the Temple and the wall after the exile by means of their announcements of salvation stand in a very old tradition of salvation prophecy which was also cult prophecy with respect to its origin.

(e) Finally, the fifth Mari letter shows two other speech forms that recur in the prophecy of Israel. One is the self-predication of God [12]:

> In an oracle Adad, the lord of Kallasu, (spoke) in the following way:
> Am I not Adad, the lord of Kallasu, who . . .

and later:

> Thus, I am the lord of the throne, earth and city; I will . . .

The sentences correspond to the frequent self-predication of God in the prophetic speech of the Old Testament, cf. Jer. 23:23 f.:

> Am I a God at hand, . . . and not a God afar off? . . .
> Do I not fill heaven and earth?

It is important that the self-predication of God is already found in the early history of prophecy within the messenger speech in this fifth Mari letter; so the self-predication of God within the prophetic speech in the Old Testament might be able to point toward the early beginnings of prophecy. Now the relation to the prophetic speech worked out by Zimmerli called the divine self-proof (*Selbsterweis*) (W. Zimmerli, " Das Wort des göttlichen Selbsterweises [*Erweiswort*], eine prophetische Gattung,"

125

Mélanges bibliques, en l'honneur de André Robert, 1957)
must be explained still more precisely; it might possibly be
that an early form of this type of speech could be found
here.

The other form is the continuation of the self-predication:

> Have I not reared him (i.e., Zimrilim) on my bosom
> and led him back to his father's throne?
> When I had led him back to the throne of his father
> I gave him, besides that, a dwelling place (i.e., a palace).

These sentences correspond exactly to the "review of
God's early saving acts" in the prophetic speeches of the
eighth and seventh centuries, e.g., Amos 2:9-11, except that
here they are saving acts for the people whereas in the
Mari letters they are only for the king. But in Nathan's
speech to David in II Sam., ch. 12, we find a remarkable
Old Testament parallel to this also. It reflects the same
kind of expansion of a prophetic announcement which
arises here and there as a form of contrast (now you are
acting against me even though I have done so much for
you!).

3. *The Relation to Prophecy in Israel.* The result of this
comparison is of particular importance for the relation of
salvation and judgment prophecy in Israel. The messages
of god in the Mari letters correspond to salvation prophecy at several important points. They show that salvation
prophecy in Israel had an earlier history in the Near East
in a type of salvation prophecy which was related to the
cult and whose addressee was the king. At the same time,
however, they show that salvation and judgment prophecy
cannot be understood by merely placing them in opposition to each other. Their relationship is much more complicated. In several of these Mari letters what is decidedly
salvation prophecy is connected to a reproach against the
king, therefore somewhat corresponding to or similar to the

prophetic accusation in Israel. This raises the possibility that also in Israel, under certain circumstances, not only judgment prophecy, but salvation prophecy as well, could be connected with a criticism of the behavior of the king. This would help us to understand more clearly, e.g., the figure of Nathan whom we encounter as a court and salvation prophet, but who makes an accusation against the king in II Sam., ch. 12. This gives the tradition of Nathan a greater historical credibility. We must therefore reckon with the possibility that the judgment prophets and those who handed down their traditions have made the description of their opponents, the salvation prophets, too one-sided (e.g., Micah 3:5). In any case, we can no longer say that the salvation prophets in Israel have only said what the king and the people wanted them to say. The conjecture of quite a few of the more recent investigators who have warned against placing the salvation and judgment prophets too sharply in opposition to one another receives a confirmation here in the Mari letters.[13]

On one point, however, their distinction is, at the same time, all the more clear and unambiguous; the unconditional announcement of ill or judgment is completely missing from the Mari letters. Even in the place where the god reproaches or accuses the king through his messenger, the conditional announcement of salvation continues to exist. The god is prevented from rendering his help at the time because of the behavior of his devotee, but as soon as this neglect is rectified his help will again be given. In the second paragraph of the fifth letter an announcement of judgment is found which seems at first to be unconditional:

Now, just as I led him back to the throne of his father's
  house,
I will take (the place) Nahlatum out of his hand!
If he will not give,
  since I am the lord of the throne, earth, and city;
I will take away what I gave!

It is not unconditional, however, for the stipulation follows it immediately. The conditional announcement of judgment is the counterpart to the conditional announcement of salvation and aims only at backing up the demand with a threat. The point of departure and the goal of the whole speech of god is the demand for an animal sacrifice.

The conditional announcement of judgment, as the counterpart to the conditional announcement of salvation, is therefore completely possible within the scope of salvation prophecy as the Mari letters show. Here another connecting link with the Old Testament announcement of judgment has been found, but it is still only a formal connecting link. With the variation of the conditional announcement of ill in the Mari letters it becomes very clear what the *unconditional* announcement of judgment running through the centuries in Israel means.

A large number of structurally parallel forms have been shown that give an important, and hitherto unknown, background to the history of the prophetic speech forms in the Old Testament. The most important result for the history and understanding of prophetic speech in the Old Testament is that the character of the prophetic speeches as *messengers' speeches* is now fully confirmed by the religio-historical background shown in the Mari letters. There is thus no longer any reason for disputing the definition of the prophetic speech introduced by Lindblom and Köhler which assumes its character to be the speech of a messenger.

C. The Prophetic Judgment-Speech to Individuals (JI)

The investigation into the Mari letters, which has placed the emphasis upon the linguistic structure of the message of god recounted in them, has led to the conclusion that the prophetic speeches of the Old Testament must have had an earlier history, a section of which is represented by these Mari letters. The stress of the inquiry into the prophetic speech forms and their history is thus shifted to the time *before* written prophecy. The speech forms that Amos, Hosea, Isaiah, and Jeremiah used could not have arisen at the same time as the prophets themselves. But what do we know of their earlier history? If we raise the question in this way, then we cannot circumvent any elements of this earlier history that are present within the Old Testament, i.e., in the historical books. When in previous research the question about the *speech forms* of the prophetic speeches which were passed down in the historical books was practically not raised at all, it is quite understandable in the light of the presupposition that was accepted then in almost all of the research. This presupposition was that "genuine" prophetic speeches could scarcely be transmitted in the historical books since they were fully imbedded in narratives and accounts that arose in a time long after the period in which these prophetic words were spoken. Nevertheless, the possibility is not excluded that the narratives of the books of the Kings, which depend in part on sources that stand very close to

129

the events, have now and then preserved prophetic speeches in such a way that their original form is still recognizable at least in outline. This possibility becomes stronger if one compares the tradition of the prophetic speeches in Kings with those in Chronicles. The versions of the prophetic speeches in Chronicles are so different from those in Kings that, because of this difference, those in Kings quite automatically give the impression of having a greater proximity to the actual prophetic speeches.

If it is now established that the forms of the prophetic speeches are much older than the prophecy of the eighth and seventh centuries, then a new basis is given for asking

I. THE STRUCTURE OF THE JUDGMENT–SPEECH TO INDIVIDUALS (JI), SHOWN IN THREE EXAMPLES

	Amos 7:16-17	I Kings 21:18-19	II Kings 1:3-4
Commissioning of the messenger:	—	Arise, go down . . . And you shall say to him, . . .	Arise, go up to meet . . . and say to them,
Summons to hear:	Now therefore hear the word of the Lord.	—	—
Accusation:	You say, " Do not prophesy . . ."	" Have you killed, and also taken possession? ". . .	" Is it because there is no God in Israel that you are going to inquire of Baalzebub . . . ? "
Messenger formula:	Therefore thus says the Lord:	" Thus says the Lord:	Now therefore thus says the Lord,
Announcement:	" Your wife shall be a harlot in the city, and your sons and your daughters . . . , and your land . . . ; you yourself . . ."	' In the place where the dogs licked up the blood of Naboth shall dogs lick up your own blood.' "	" You shall not come down from the bed to which you have gone, but you shall surely die."

130

whether elements of this earlier history are contained in the accounts found in Kings. One is then to begin with the forms as they are found in the reliable tradition of the prophetic books.

In the account in Amos 7:10-17, vs. 16 and 17 contain a prophetic announcement of judgment directed to an individual. The structure of this speech, which is recorded within an account, is the simplest imaginable, so simple, in fact, that it arises naturally out of the situation that was reported:

Summons to hear
Accusation
Introduction to the announcement by the message formula (with " therefore ")
Announcement of judgment (in personal address)

As the diagram shows, both of the examples of a judgment-speech to an individual in Kings have the same structure. Again, in both passages, the structure arises naturally out of the situation of the report. It is the same event in all three passages that gives rise to the same form of speech in all three. From the viewpoint of the history of forms, we have before us the most propitious case imaginable, in that a well-defined speech form is passed down along with the situation to which it belongs and out of which it grew. The example in I Kings 21:18-19 shows this situation the most impressively. A crime has occurred — the execution of an innocent person. The one who committed the crime is the king. Since formally this deed adhered to the legal procedure no one intervened. There is as well no higher authority capable of intervening against the king. In this case then, God himself intervenes. He does this by commissioning a messenger, the prophet Elijah, to confront the king to expose his deed, and to announce the judgment of God to him. This situation and this commission result in the prophetic word, and the delivery of this speech is now reported. In the speech form that corresponds clearly and

131

exactly to this incident this speech brings together with utmost pregnancy and conciseness that which has taken place and the decision of God which is pertinent to it. Of course, the situation in each of these speeches is somewhat different, and so none of these speeches of God to individuals is completely like the others; that is true with every living speech form. The agreement of the speeches in Amos with the examples from Kings in the main features of the situation, as well as the speech form which grew out of it, makes it possible to assume the existence of an established form which must now be investigated further.

The most important formal characteristics are furnished by the three examples already named:

1. The presupposition of the utterance of a JI is a transgression by the one to whom the speech is directed and, specifically, a transgression in which no one intervenes. The JI is not concerned with general corruption or wickedness, or the like, but its presupposition is without exception a concrete individual event which has just occurred. The circle that is encompassed by the occurrence of the prophetic speech is temporally and spatially small.

2. The JI has two parts; it contains an accusation and an announcement. Only these two together constitute the messenger's speech; both have their existence only as members of the whole. But God's word, in the proper sense, is only the announcement. It is designated as such by the introductory messenger formula (with " therefore ") ; the accusation stands *before* the real messenger's speech.[1]

3. The true word of God, the announcement of judgment, is *one* sentence consisting of a simple, direct announcement of a catastrophic future spoken plainly to the addressee in a personal address and introduced as the word of God by the messenger formula.

4. The announcement of judgment is based upon an accusation. It consists of the mere statement of factual evidence. In Amos, ch. 7, it takes the form of an assertion [2]; in I Kings, ch. 21, and II Kings, ch. 1, the form of an ac-

cusing question: "Have you killed, and also taken possession?" It is a statement for which a particular revelation is not required. The factual evidence established in these sentences might also be established or detected by others.

Shortness is characteristic of the JI. The announcement and accusation each have one part.

5. The relation of the announcement and the accusation to each other is effected very simply in these short, early prophetic speeches. In view of the facts presented in the accusation, the prophet personally sets these forth immediately and directly before the accused. For this reason, a logical linguistic connection of accusation and announcement (by "because" and the like) is not yet needed. Because of the proximity to the facts, both parts of these speeches are able to stand next to each other unconnected. This accounts, as well, for the shortness of both parts of this speech.

In addition to the formal characteristics, there is also the analysis of the content of the proceeding. In I Kings, ch. 21, and II Kings, ch. 1, the prophet appears as an accuser where a transgression was committed and no one has begun proceedings against it. In both cases it is the king before whom the prophet appears as accuser; there is no higher authority who can make an accusation against the king. In both cases the transgression is the breach of an old law of God; Ahab (I Kings, ch. 21) had transgressed the law forbidding killing (Ex. 21:12); Ahaziah (II Kings, ch. 1) had transgressed the law forbidding the turning to other gods (Ex. 23:13).[3]

When the prophet steps before the king as an accuser, nothing different happens here — if at first one looks only at the word of accusation — than would have happened in making an accusation in the regular legal procedure. That is a great deal clearer in both of these speeches than in a judgment-speech addressed to the nation because: (1) in both, the accused is an individual person; (2) in both, the accusation points out a single transgression that has just

133

happened. Both correspond exactly to the regular judicial procedure, (3) it is treated as a transgression against the current law in Israel.

Thus it is shown that each of these examples is treated as a single accusation in the prophetic judgment-speech, an accusation that conforms to the regular judicial procedure in three essential points.

The statement of the accusation must have been followed by the convening of the judicial body and the determination and proclamation of the decision. This is not a possibility here because there is no one who convenes such a judicial body against the king, and, moreover, the prophet does not have *this* commission. Rather, God himself — God as judge — appears here in place of the higher court which could render a decision. God, then, watches over the law and he can demand that the king stand before judgment. It is God, therefore, who hands down the decision about the accused.

The prophet has to transmit this decision of God to the accused; he is the messenger who brings the decision that was handed down by God before the accused — in this case the king — and proclaims it to him. The " proclamation of the decision " is carried out, not by the judge himself, but by the messenger of the judge. For that reason, it is introduced with the messenger formula by virtue of which the messenger possesses full authority.

The decision that he proclaims to the accused names the punishment of God for the transgression of which he is accused. The punishment of death was demanded by the old law of God for both transgressions in the two examples and, in both cases, the prophet accordingly announces the death of the king involved. While this corresponds to the regular judgment procedure an essential distinction remains in that the one proclaiming the divine decision is *only* a messenger and in no sense has executive power. This is seen in that at first, nothing at all happened to the accused to whom the punishment of God was proclaimed;

134

he can even start a procedure against the messenger of the judge, for the messenger is completely powerless. The decision of God, i.e., the punishment, does not occur on the spot (it is therefore something different in nature from the curse), but it is announced for a later point in time. Both ways in which the utterance of the prophetic judgment-speech to the individual deviates from the regular judgment procedure belong together by nature: (*a*) the judge does not proclaim the decision in person but through a messenger whom he commissions for this purpose; (*b*) the decision is not enforced when it is announced, but rather, the execution of the punishment is announced for a later time.

In addition to the three points listed above in which the utterance of the prophetic judgment-speech to the individual agrees with the regular judgment procedure, there is still another: (4) the announcement of judgment corresponds to the proclamation of the decision in the court. The places where it deviates from this were shown above. But this deviation is relatively slight inasmuch as the arc that stretches from the proclamation of the decision to its execution is smaller in comparison with the later judgment-speeches to the people. In fact, temporally, it stretches over only a few years so that the occurrence of that which the prophet announced is experienced by the witnesses and the parties concerned in the speech; spatially, it concerns a single person so that the whole event does not step very far out of the framework of the regular judicial procedure. The single essential distinction is that, in this case, God appears in the place of the judge as the representative of the national community, and the punishment that is announced by him through his messenger does not occur immediately; on the contrary, nothing at all happens at first to the condemned person.

In the four points just cited one can see the close proximity that the prophetic judgment-speech addressed to an individual has to the regular judicial procedure. It actually arises out of the situation that is reported in all of these JI; it is a transgression that has been committed against the old law instituted by God on which the covenant between God and the people rested. Since no one had started proceedings against the one who committed the crime, God himself intervenes through his messenger.

Its division into two parts is thus shown to be characteristic of its nature on the basis of the proceeding out of which it grew. Just as the accusation and announcement of punishment belong to the regular judicial procedure as basic elements, they belong, as well, to the prophetic judgment-speech to the individual. Actually, an allowance for this division into two parts has already been made in the old legal maxims where an offense sets the proceedings in motion:

> Ex. 21:12: Whoever strikes a man so that he dies shall be put to death.

Exactly the same definition is repeated in the two parts of Elijah's speech to Ahab!

It is then not necessary to assume — at least with regard to the prophetic speech — that its origin was in the cultic act of judgment. Its proximity to the regular judgment procedure and to the old law of God is obvious. In regard to Würthwein's thesis it should be noted at this point that the passage which he cites out of The Psalms never mentions a judgment of God against an individual. The cultic origin of the prophetic judgment-speech which he supposes would, therefore, have to be limited to the judgment-speeches against the people. I agree with H. W. Wolff, however, in that the origin of the prophetic judgment-speech *generally* is to be sought in the regular legal procedure.[4] " The origin of the style form of a part of this citation can be perceived in the legal life. One of the origins of the citation is the legal life." (P. 62.) " The lawsuit procedure is the stylistic background of the prophetic citation." (P. 69.)[5]

136

II. THE JUDGMENT–SPEECH TO INDIVIDUALS IN THE OLD TESTAMENT

These texts, which agree in structure, make it possible to determine what is certainly an early, very simple form of the prophetic judgment-speech to an individual person.

The Old Testament does not contain many such prophetic judgment-speeches (or announcements of ill) to individuals.

In the historical books:

I Sam. 2:27-36; (3:11-14); 13:11-14; 15:10-31; II Sam., ch. 12
I Kings 11:29-40; 13:1-3; 14:7-14; 17:1; 20:35-43; 21:17-22; 22:13-23
II Kings 1:6(16); 20:14-19; 21:10-15
I Chron.; II Chron. Cf. the excursus.
(See also Ex. 4:21-23: Moses to Pharaoh.)

In the prophetic books:

Amos 7:14-17
Isa. (7:10-16); 22:15-25; 37:22-30; 38:1 (= II Kings 20:1); 39:3-7 (= II Kings 20:14-19)
Jer. 20:1-6; 22:10-12, 13-19, 24-27 (28), 30; 28:12-16; (29:21-23); 29:24-32; 36:29-30; 37:17
Ezek. (17:11-21)

All the prophetic announcements of judgment in the books of Kings are, without exception, directed to an individual person and never to a group or a class, or the whole nation or other nations! It is in the writing prophets that we first find the announcement of judgment to the nation.[5a] The collection and transmission of prophetic speeches first began with these; correspondingly, almost all the judgment-speeches to individuals in the prophetic books are found in

137

narrative texts (Amos 7:10-17; Jer. 36:27-31; Baruch's account in Jeremiah).

After Jeremiah, judgment-speeches to an individual person are no longer encountered.[5b] They are missing also from Hosea, Micah, Zephaniah, and (with the exception mentioned) Ezekiel.[6] A decline can be clearly recognized. The JI had its proper time in the period of the kings *before* the writing prophets. The prophetic judgment-speech (that is found only in a narrative context), which has come down to us from this time, is exclusively a judgment-speech to the individual and almost always to the king. A few examples extend into the time of the writing prophets only to disappear completely after that.

This results in the positive conclusion, with respect to the history of the prophetic speech, that the judgment-speeches directed against an individual person are an older type than those directed against the whole nation (or a group within it).

It is not judgment prophecy as such that begins with Amos, but rather *the announcement of judgment to the entire nation.* This gave the announcement of judgment its own significance which caused a *special* tradition of these speeches to be established independent of their former setting in the historical narratives. Here, an important turning point in the history of God with his people can be seen. The sins of the nation as a whole, as the transgressions of the " corporate personality," had acquired such a significance that the commission of the prophet to intervene as the messenger from the court of God in case of a transgression (particularly of the king) is no longer sufficient. The accusation must now be made against the entire nation and the judicial decision of God announced to all the people.

The passages in which the JI is encountered shall be investigated below, first, by explaining two speeches from the previous examples which resemble one another very little, and then, by looking at the components of the prophetic speeches in the whole group. It is to be noted in ad-

138

vance concerning the text that not too much can be built on the basis of the wording since the prophetic speeches have been absorbed more or less into the narratives. Nevertheless, it seems possible to me to assume that in any case, the sequence of the motifs in the majority of the texts corresponds to the original prophetic speeches.

The agreement of the three previously investigated prophetic speeches in the five points indicated can serve as a point of departure for inquiring into other corresponding speeches. This should be shown, first, in two obscure examples. The first, II Sam., ch. 12, varies from the form of the JI which was found inasmuch as it is completely embedded in a narrative in which, at first glance, the original prophetic word seems to be unobtainable. Beyond that, it is temporally quite far removed from the previous examples since it goes back to the beginning of the period of the kingdom. The other example is obscure inasmuch as it is composed in the characteristic language of one of the great writing prophets and one can hardly assume, on first glance, that it belongs to the early form of the judgment-speech to the individual.

II Sam., ch. 12 — the speech of Nathan to David:

(Here, of course, the prophetic speech is no longer couched in its original form, but is absorbed by an extensive narrative. Nevertheless, the elements of the original speech can still be recognized.)

(a) The messenger-commissioning is transformed in the narrative:

And the Lord sent Nathan to David. (V. 1.)

(b) The accusing question:

Why have you despised the word of the Lord, to do what is evil in his sight? (V. 9a.)

The statement of the evidence:

You have smitten Uriah the Hittite with the sword, and have taken his wife to be your wife. (V. 9b.)

139

(c) The announcement of judgment introduced by the messenger formula:

> Thus says the Lord, " Behold, I will raise up evil against you out of your own house; and I will take your wives before your eyes." (V. 11.)

These sentences contain the elements of a judgment-speech directed to the individual; in this revised form one cannnot expect a literal repetition. Verse 9a cannot belong to the original prophetic speech, for the early prophetic speeches are never so general and theological. Following this comes a whole series of repetitions and expansions; it is quite possible that the speech of Nathan was transmitted to the narrator in two or even more forms and he wanted to preserve as much as possible in his narrative (v. 9a = 9c; 10b = 9; two announcements in vs. 10a and 11). It is possible that vs. 7b-8 contain an element of the original speech: an expansion of the accusation through the contrast of this accusation with God's earlier treatment of the accused. This is a motif frequently found in the later prophetic speeches. That this was already a possibility in the speech of Nathan to David is seen in a further parallel in the Mari letters to be discussed below. This short form of the prophetic judgment-speech appears, as well, in Isa., ch. 22:

15: Thus says the Lord God of hosts,
    " Come, go to this steward, to Shebna . . .
16: " What have you to do here and whom have you here,
    that you have hewn here a tomb for yourself,
    you who hew a tomb on the height,
    and carve a habitation for yourself in the rock?
17: " Behold, the Lord will hurl you away violently, O you strong man.
18: " He will seize firm hold on you, and whirl you round and round, and throw you like a ball into a wide land; there you shall die, and there shall be your splendid chariots, you shame of your master's house."

140

Even if this speech is essentially more developed and broader than the first example, the originally short form can still be recognized. 1. The speech is introduced by the commissioning of a messenger and deals with a message to an individual. The commissioning is shortened in that the second part, " and say to him," is missing, probably because of the reproachful tone of the commssion.

2. There is an exact formal correspondence as well as a material correspondence between the accusation and the accusing question Elijah directs to Ahab in I Kings 21:19. Here also this accusing question states the evidence which is again available to anyone, and which requires no revelation to establish. Verse 16b trails along after this only ineptly repeating it; the forceful directness of the accusing question in v. 16a is abandoned. Either these participles in v. 16b are a secondary expansion (which could well be from Isaiah) or — and this is more probable — v. 16b is to be read before v. 16a as a more detailed description of " this steward "; the participle is much more suitable here and its place would then correspond exactly to the sentence in I Kings 21:18b, where in the *introduction* of the prophetic speech there is also a more detailed description.

3. The announcement of salvation is broader than in I Kings 21:19b, but not broader than Amos 7:17. There is an essential difference, however, in that this announcement has two parts; this is usually a characteristic of the announcement to the nation. The intervention of God in v. 17, is " Behold, the Lord will hurl . . ." and its consequence, " there you shall die, and there . . . ." To that extent, Isa. 22:15-18 does not represent the pure type of short speech; one can notice that in the announcement there is an approximation to the later long form.

4. One can tell the short form in that a grammatical connection between the reason and the announcement is missing. The accusing question stands completely on its own in v. 16a; then, in v. 17, the " Behold " (which stands

141

very frequently in the position of the messenger form) introduces the announcement with no connection to what went before.

III. THE PARTS OF THE JUDGMENT–SPEECH TO INDIVIDUALS

1. *Introduction.* An investigation of the introductory phrases in this group does not seem to me to be worthwhile because, as components of the narrative in the historical texts, they are almost always formulated by the narrator so that they can scarcely belong to the original prophetic speech. The introduction is ordinarily the commissioning of a messenger, but this can be formulated in quite different ways. It can, e.g., be transformed entirely into a narrative as in II Sam. 12:1: "And the Lord sent Nathan to David."

Accompanying this, there can also be a summons to hear as in Amos 7:16; II Kings 20:16; Jer. 28:15; Isa. 7:13.

2. *The Accusation.* (a) The first accusations to be considered are those (I Kings 21:18; II Kings 1:3) which correspond to the examples cited at the outset of this study. Exactly the same form is encountered again and again:

> Isa. 7:13: Hear then, O house of David!
> Is it too little for you to weary men,
> that you weary my God also?
> I Sam. 2:29: Why then look with greedy eye at my sacrifices . . . ?

> II Sam. 12:9a: Why have you despised the word of the Lord,
> to do what is evil in his sight?
> Isa. 22:16: What have you to do here and whom have you here, that you have hewn here a tomb for yourself . . . ?

142

37:23: Whom have you mocked and reviled? . . .
the Holy One of Israel!
24: and you have said . . .
29: Because you have raged against me . . . .
Jer. 22:15: Do you think you are a king because you
compete in cedar?
Did not your father eat and drink and do
justice and righteousness?
17: But you have eyes and heart only for your
dishonest gain,
for shedding innocent blood, and for prac-
ticing oppression and violence.

Isaiah 22:16 and Jer. 22:15 correspond exactly to the examples. Here we are able to assume that these words were
spoken to the accused face-to-face and were committed to
writing so exactly that they confront us today as they were
spoken.[7] Isaiah 37:23 also belongs to this group. But one
can see here a very significant expansion: Following the
accusing question in v. 23 comes a citation in v. 24 that il-
lustrates the "mocking" and "reviling" (v. 23). Otherwise, the accusation in this form always has only one part.
When the accusation here is illustrated with a citation of
the accused, the reason for this is that Isaiah cannot come
into the immediate presence of the accused — it is the
king, Sennacherib — and so he "quotes" him. This means
that he uses the citation to make the offense present in his
accusation. When the accusation, "Because you have raged
against me and your arrogance has come to my ears," appears again in v. 29, it is merely a literary reiteration
caused by the wide interval between its prior occurrence
and the announcement which only now follows.

II Samuel 12:9a is also a literary construction and not
the original accusation. This follows in v. 9b in the declaratory form. When it is expanded in v. 9a with an accusing
question, one can see how the narrator formed this supple-
mentary sentence out of a correct understanding of the
form of the accusing question which belongs here. The lit-

143

erary construction of v. 9a is recognizable in the general theological concepts.

Belonging to this group are also the passages in which the accusing question can be recognized, but which do not explicitly name the transgression:

> I Sam. 13:11: Samuel said, "What have you done?"
> 15:14: And Samuel said, "What then is this bleating of sheep in my ears . . . ?"
> 23: Because you have rejected the word of the Lord . . .
> II Kings 20:14 f.: (Isaiah questions Hezekiah about the situation)
> What did these men say? . . .
> What have they seen in your house?

A precise accusation is not formulated in any of these passages. In the questions, however (one could compare them with the questions in a hearing), the facts of the matter are established which give the grounds for the accusation. They do not need to be stated explicitly, for in the course of the narrative it becomes clear that an accusation is implicit in the facts that were exposed in the questions. Even if a firmly established form can no longer be recognized in all three places and the narrator composes quite freely, one may still conclude from II Kings, ch. 20, that the prophetic accusation to an individual person was often a matter of the prophet's establishing the facts of the case through questions exactly as it occurs in the regular judicial process. All three places are actually similar to a hearing in which the prophet is one who hears and the king is the one heard.[8]

The form of the accusing question is also present in the Mari letters (letter 1):

> Why do the emissaries of Zimrilim not constantly linger before me
> And why has he not brought a complete (over everything) report back to me?

144

(b) Instead of an accusing question, the accusation is also formulated as a declaratory sentence; the accusation consists of a mere statement.

II Sam. 12:9b: You have smitten Uriah the Hittite with the sword, and have taken his wife to be your wife.

I Kings 14:9: But you have done evil . . . and made for yourself other gods . . .

Amos 7:16: You say, " Do not prophesy against Israel."

Jer. 28:13: You have broken wooden bars.

15b: The Lord has not sent you, and you have made this people trust in a lie.

29:25: You [Shemaiah of Nehelam] have sent letters in your name.

36:29: You [Jehoiakim] have burned this scroll, saying . . .

29:21: Concerning Ahab . . . and Zedekiah . . . , who are prophesying a lie to you in my name . . .

23: They have committed adultery with their neighbors' wives, and they have spoken in my name lying words which I did not command them.

This second form of the accusation is found somewhat more frequently than the first; in regard to content, it corresponds completely with the first. (The noteworthy fact might also be mentioned here that the accusation in the " accusation of God " in the Psalms of Lamentation is also found in the form of a question [Why? How long?] and a statement that have the same meaning and stand side by side.) [9]

One could not imagine a speech form any simpler than the one found in these sentences. It consists of a simple statement in the second person singular perfect without introduction and without connectives. We can be completely certain that we have discovered a basic form here that has absolutely no earlier historical development. An-

145

other indication of this is that this accusation in the form of a declaratory sentence has remained unchanged all the way from the early traditions to Jeremiah:

> II Sam. 12:9b: You have smitten Uriah the Hittite with the sword.
> Jer. 36:29: You have burned this scroll, saying . . .

It is exactly the same in Jer. 29:25; 28:15b. This simple statement of the facts is sufficient to support the judgment decision that then follows. These sentences agree completely with the profane accusation which is in the form of a declaratory sentence.

> I Kings 21:10: And set two base fellows opposite him, and let them bring a charge against him, saying, " You have cursed God and the king."
> (Cf. Jer. 26:11; Dan. 3:12.)

Without going farther, it is already clear here that this speech form stems from the regular judicial procedure.[9a] These lapidary statements in the accusation completely correspond to the apodictic laws; these are also formulated in the second person singular although as prohibitions in the imperfect with *lō'*. The statement " You have cursed God and the king " establishes the breach of the commandment: Ex. 22:28, " You shall not revile God, nor curse a ruler of your people." In the correspondence to the apodictic law and in the agreement with the profane accusation, this form shows that the meaning and function of the accusation against an individual is the maintenance of the law of God in the cases where this law is broken and the offender is not punished.

A special case is formed by the accusations that do not presuppose an old law and therefore cannot simply assert that there was a transgression against such a law (as in II Sam. 12:9b). That is the case where the transgression consists of an attempt to silence the word of the prophet. This is found frequently in the following group of passages: Amos 7:16; (Jer. 20:2) ; Jer. 28:13; 36:29. In both

146

places in Jeremiah, this transgression consists of an act of destruction (the breaking of the yoke, the burning of the book) which can be stated simply. In Amos 7:16 no direct accusation in the second person is expressed; the hindrance of the prophetic word is only stated in apposition to the address: "You, you who say . . ." The possibility is not to be excluded that this relative sentence was added when it was placed into written form. Such a possibility is also present in Jer. 20:2; it is almost the same situation, only intensified by the fact that Pashhur had Jeremiah placed in the stocks overnight. Here the situation itself is the kind that expresses the accusation in such a way that a formulation of the accusation seems superfluous. The prophetic speech in Jer. 20:2 contains *only* the announcement of judgment, no accusation, and yet the basis of the judgment given Pashhur is completely clear. Here the most extreme intensification of the prophetic judgment-speech to an individual is found. An essential characteristic of it is that the accusation is made in personal confrontation and in the immediate presence of the evidence. Here in Jer. 20:2 the evidence is so immediate and conclusive that a formal accusation can be omitted.

Also in the affair concerning false or lying prophecy (Jer. 28:15b; 29:25, 21, 23b) no law is cited because there is no objective criterion. Thus, the formulations of the accusation here are less firmly fixed and to some extent, secondary developments as in Jer. 28:15b; 29:21, 23. This represents a subsequent literary formulation of the accusation; sometimes it can also be changed into the third person.

Nothing more of the original form of the accusation in I Kings 14:9 can be recognized; the whole prophetic speech from vs. 7-11 is a Deuteronomic formulation.

The same holds true, by and large, for a third group of formulations of the accusation which here — in contrast to the original form — are brought into a logical-grammatical connection with the accusation.

147

I Sam. 15:23:	Because you have rejected the word of the Lord . . .
I Kings 20:36:	Because you have not obeyed the voice of the Lord . . .
42:	Because you have let go out of your hand the man whom I had devoted to destruction . . .
II Kings 21:11:	Because Manasseh . . . has committed these abominations, and has done things more wicked than . . . and has made Judah also to sin with his idols . . .

In I Sam. 15:23 and Isa. 37:29 these causal sentences supplement the accusation that was previously formulated directly and in a declaratory sentence. In other places the whole accusation is worded in the form of a declaratory sentence. Thus the mere causal wording of a concrete accusation that establishes a single, definite transgression as I Kings 20:42 — in this case the sentence could have preserved the original accusation which then was uttered in the declaratory sentence — must again be distinguished from a general theological-conceptual accusation such as I Sam. 15:23; I Kings 20:36; II Kings 21:11; and Isa. 37:29(?). These are certainly literary formulations in which the person giving the report still knows only the *fact* that there has been an accusation made. A definite accusation was no longer available to him (almost all the examples of this group come out of narrative texts).

Within this form we can therefore recognize the clear features of a history of the prophetic accusation directed to an individual. Its course goes from the accusation which is issued in a single completely isolated sentence (a declaration or accusing question) to one that is causally connected with the announcement; in regard to content, this goes from an accusation that establishes a single definite transgression to one that is generally and conceptually formulated.

3. *The Announcement*

(a) The Introduction of the Announcement

While the accusation is given most of the time without having any introduction, the announcement is introduced as the word of Yahweh. Here, the evidence clearly indicates that in the word of God to an individual, the announcement is the real word of God.

The most frequent introduction is *lākēn kô 'āmar yhwh* or a variation of this messenger formula: I Sam. 2:30; I Kings 21:19; Amos 7:1; Jer. 22:18; 28:16; 29:32; 36:30; instead of *lākēn, kî:* Jer. 22:11; 20;3; I Kings 11:31; merely, *kô 'āmar yhwh:* II Sam. 12:7b (in the beginning) ; I Kings 14:7; 20:42; II Kings 20:1; Jer. 22:30; only *lākēn:* I Kings 14:10; II Kings 1:6; or merely *wᵉ:* Isa. 37:29 f. Appearing in the place of the messenger formula can be, " therefore behold ": I Kings 14:10, or only " behold ": II Sam. 12:11; I Kings II:31; 13:2; 20:36; Jer. 20:3; 29:21; or " Behold, the days are coming": II Kings 20:16.

An introduction is missing only where the prophetic speech is completely embedded in the narrative as in I Sam. 13:13 f.; 15:16 ff.; II Sam., ch. 12. One will hardly be able to draw any general conclusions from this evidence; the only certain result is that the announcement is predominantly introduced by the messenger formula and is thereby designated as the real word of God. In addition, a distinction should be made between the formula *kô 'āmar yhwh,* which introduces the *whole* speech, and *lākēn kô 'āmar yhwh,* which introduces the announcement.

(b) The Form of the Announcement

In the speeches in which it seems probable that the original form has been approximately preserved, the announcement has one part: I Kings 21:19; II Kings 1:6; and Amos 7:16 (see above) .

In addition to the passages above are I Sam. 13:13 f.; I Kings 20:36, 42; II Kings 20:1, 16; Isa. 7:17; Jer. 22:11 f., 18 f., 30. To say that it has one part means here that the announcement consists of only a statement about the pun-

149

ishment that is to befall the person to whom the speech is directed. That is certainly the earlier form of the announcement of judgment in which the one giving the announcement confronts the other person involved face-to-face. In the announcement to the people a differentiation has taken place: before the actual notice of punishment, the " intervention of God " appears in a sentence as a speech by God in the first person.

This form of the announcement which has two parts is found in a few JI (announcements of judgment to individuals) : I Sam. 2:30-34; II Sam. 12:11 ff.; I Kings 14:7-11; (Isa. 22:17-19; 37:29 f.) ; Jer. 20:4; 28:16; 29:21; 29:32.

Examples:

Jer. 28:16: Therefore thus says the Lord:
        " Behold, I will remove you from the face of the earth.
        This very year you shall die."
  20:4: Behold, I will make you a terror to yourself and to all your friends. They shall fall by the sword of their enemies while you look on.

All these announcements of judgment having two parts can be explained as secondary mixed forms. It is, for example, completely certain that this is the case in Jer. 36:30-31:

Therefore thus says the Lord concerning Jehoiakim king of Judah,
He shall have none to sit upon the throne of David,
    and his dead body shall be cast out to the heat . . . .
And I will punish him and his offspring
    and his servants for their iniquity.

Here it is clear that the last sentence, the intervention of God, has been appended; the language of this sentence sufficiently proves that. However, this is not so clear everywhere. Even if one reckons in each case with a literary construction in the two-part announcement analogous to the later form, the frequent occurrence of the speech of God

150

in this group is still remarkable. Some of the formulations found there give the impression of being completely original as Isa. 37:29:

Because you [Sennacherib] have raged against me . . .
I will put my hook in your nose
 and my bit in your mouth,
and I will turn you back on the way by which you came.

In contrast with all the other places, the concern here is with an enemy king. His transgression is something essentially different from that of which the Israelite kings are accused; it simply consists of his inimical actions against Israel and is, therefore, a transgression only from Israel's viewpoint. A more precise examination shows that the whole speech against Sennacherib is not an announcement of judgment but only appears in the guise of one; it is actually a salvation-speech by Isaiah to Hezekiah, who in distress over Sennacherib had come before Yahweh; Isaiah speaks and acts here in the function of an intercessor as a salvation prophet. That is confirmed by a parallel out of the Mari letters which attracts our attention here:

Then I will make the chiefs of the Benjaminites
wriggle in a fisherman's basket and put them down before you!

This similar metaphor has the same function of underscoring an announcement of salvation.

The same holds true also for Isa. 22:17-19, a speech delivered against a *foreign* official:

Behold, the Lord will hurl you away violently, O you strong man.
He will seize firm hold on you, and whirl you round and round, and throw you like a ball into a wide land; there you shall die, and there shall be your splendid chariots, you shame of your master's house.

Both speeches, Isa. 22:17-19 and 37:29 f., are then related to a completely different tradition; they stand in the

151

line of salvation prophecy in which an intervention of God was described (*a*) in the form of the speech of God in the first person and (*b*) in strong, prodigious metaphors as the overwhelming action of God against the enemies.

Jer. 22:24-27, especially v. 26, sounds remarkably like Isa. 22:17 f.:

> Jer. 22:26: I will hurl you and the mother . . . into another country . . . and there you shall die.

One can assume that this announcement is influenced by the form which speaks in the first person of the intervention of God against Israel's enemies. Earlier in the same Mari letter this intervention of god against the enemies is described in fixed phraseology which is characteristic of the holy war in Israel: " I give into your hand . . ." This sentence, somewhat modified, occurs also in Jer. 22:24-27:

> 25: . . . and [I] give you into the hand of those who seek your life . . . .

(Found also in Jer. 29:21; 37:17.) Also the occurrence of this sentence — which is actually not appropriate for an individual since originally it was always directed to a group — suggests that it has been influenced by salvation-speeches in which Yahweh spoke in the first person.

In any case, then, the extraordinary number of places in which the announcement of the JI has two parts will be explained not only as the subsequent accommodation to the later two-part forms; the possibility of the converging of two genuine forms will also have to be considered. The notice of punishment in the JI has, in many cases, included an " I "-speech (the " I " is God) which originated in the announcement of salvation. Beyond this, one can ask whether in general the later two-part form of the announcement of judgment —

Intervention of God (first person)
Effects of the intervention of God (third person; notice of punishment) —

has not come into existence as a result of this connection. This conjecture receives some support from an observation in the historical books which points in the same direction. It should be stated here first that Würthwein's thesis that the writing prophets (he has only proved it for Amos) might have previously been salvation prophets (at least to some extent) has received further support from our investigation of the announcement. At least Isa. 22:17-19 and 37:29 f. were shown to be standing in the same line of tradition as the prophetic announcement of salvation; it probably influenced Jer. 22:24-27 and perhaps other passages.

(c) What Is Announced?

In both of the examples, I Kings 21:19 and II Kings 1:6, death is announced to the king as punishment for his transgression. The same happens in I Kings 20:42 (also in ch. 20:36, but in a legendary extension); Jer. 28:16; 29:21; Ezek. 17:16. In these passages nothing happens in the utterance of the prophetic speech that is different from what takes place in the delivery of a judge's speech. Here, the prophet says only what is necessary, i.e., what the higher court was supposed to have said but failed to say. The speech that has been given to the prophet is not anything extraordinary, but just what is demanded by the situation. In this group of speeches one may see how simple this very elementary form of the prophetic judgment-speech is, how little it goes beyond what is normal, and how self-evident it is. Here, nothing out of the ordinary in any way was revealed to the prophets; that which characterizes the prophetic speech is not found in the " what " of what was said, but solely in the " that," and in the particular time in which it was said.[10] Reference might also be made here to the decidedly profane language of these short sayings; it is thus improbable that the origin of the prophetic judgment-speech was in the cult, because the profane judgment procedure is reflected in its language and style while not a trace of cultic language can be found.

A further announcement refers to the dispossession of the kingdom.

> I Sam. 13:14: But now your kingdom shall not continue;
> . . .
> 15:28: The Lord has torn the kingdom of Israel from you this day, and has given it to a neighbor of yours.
> 23: Because you have rejected the word of the Lord, he has also rejected you from being king.
> I Kings 11:31: Behold, I am about to tear the kingdom from the hand of Solomon, and will give you ten tribes.

Even if a fixed form can no longer be recognized behind these very different sentences, the event is still clear: the king is denied the kingdom because of a transgression. That does not take place in an act of violence (such as a revolution), however, but in a mere announcement. In contrast to the foregoing groups where the punishment of death was announced, there is something essentially different here; the announcement of punishment cannot presuppose an old law that holds good for all of the members of the nation. The prophetic abjudication of the kingdom is rather an event within the new structure of the state; there must also be new standards of judgment, therefore, which are valid for the office of the king alone that furnish the basis for this decision.

In II Sam., ch. 12, neither the death punishment nor the dispossession of the kingdom appears. The announcement of punishment is:

> II Sam. 12:11: Thus says the Lord, " Behold, I will raise up evil against you out of your own house; and I will take your wives before your eyes, and give them to your neighbor, and he shall lie with your wives in the sight of this sun."

154

And there is another form:

> 12:10: Now therefore the sword shall never depart from your house.

Corresponding to this is the speech about Jeroboam:

> I Kings 14:10: Therefore behold, I will bring evil upon the house of Jeroboam, and will cut off from Jeroboam every male, both bond and free in Israel, and will utterly consume the house of Jeroboam, as a man burns up dung until it is all gone.
>
> Jer. 36:30: Therefore thus says the Lord concerning Jehoiakim king of Judah, He shall have none to sit upon the throne of David.

There are passages that are reminiscent of this announcement of judgment affecting the *house* of the person concerned: Isa. 7:14; Jer. 22:30; 29:32 (two prophets).

Quite similar is the announcement about Eli the priest:

> I Sam. 2:31: Behold, the days are coming, when I will cut off your strength and the strength of your father's house, so that there will not be an old man in your house.
>
> 34: And this which shall befall your two sons, Hophni and Phinehas, shall be a sign to you.

Here also it is hardly possible to work out a fixed form. The agreements are nevertheless so clear that the existence of such a form must be assumed. The evidence for that is: (*a*) this announcement is given to one who stands in a hereditary office (priest or king); (*b*) the punishment is executed, therefore, on the house of the person concerned, i.e., on his descendants. That the person himself is punished by this is clear from the Old Testament way of viewing life in a chain of generations.

(d) The Contrast Motif

From the context of II Sam., ch. 12, it is clear that this announcement of judgment is related to the promise of

155

Nathan in II Sam., ch. 7, in that it has in some sense been spoken in opposition to it. The speaker in both places is the same. But even without II Sam., ch. 7, coming before it, the speech itself shows this relationship.

II Sam. 12:7b: Thus says the Lord, the God of Israel, " I anointed you king over Israel, and I delivered you out of the hand of Saul;

8: and I gave you your master's house, and your master's wives into your bosom, and gave you the house of Israel and of Judah; and if this were too little, I would add to you as much more.

9: Why have you . . . ? "

The same contrast is seen in I Sam., ch. 2:

I Sam. 2:30: Therefore the Lord the God of Israel declares: " I promised that your house and the house of your father should go in and out before me for ever"; but now the Lord declares . . .

It recurs repeatedly:

I Sam. 13:13 f.: You have not kept the commandment of the Lord your God, which he commanded you; for now the Lord would have established your kingdom . . . for ever. But now . . .

15:17 f.: Though you are little in your own eyes, are you not the head of the tribes of Israel? The Lord anointed you king. . . . And the Lord sent you . . . .

19: Why then did you . . . ?

I Kings 14:7 f.: Thus says the Lord, the God of Israel: " Because I exalted you from among the people, and made you leader over my people Israel, and tore the kingdom away from the house of David and gave it to you; and yet you . . . ;

10: therefore . . ."

Jer. 22:24b: Though Coniah the son of Jehoiakim, king of Judah, were the signet ring on my right hand . . .

156

Other than Jer. 22:24, which contains only a reminiscence of the motif, all these passages are in the historical books. This means that the possibility must be considered that the prophetic speeches in these passages are not reproduced in their original form; certainty about the wording cannot be attained in any of them. This remarkable agreement, nevertheless, cannot be traced back only to the respective narrators. The motif here contrasts the offense of which the party is accused with the fact that he has been installed in his office by Yahweh and has been the recipient of other beneficial deeds. Behind this frequently recurring motif there must be an old motif that belongs to the accusation speech of the prophets. A motif such as the contrasting of the accusation with the earlier saving deeds of God for his people as in Amos 2:9-16 is well known in the later form of the JN. It might still be possible theoretically that this motif in the prophetic speeches from the books of Kings could be a literary extension of the later form by the narrator. Evidence against this, other than the agreement of the five passages, is offered by a striking parallel in the Mari letters to II Sam. 12:7-8.

	II Sam. 12:7-8
Am I not Adad, the lord of Kallasu, have I not reared him in my bosom and led him back to his father's throne? When I had led him back to the throne of his father I gave him, besides that, a dwelling place.	Thus says the Lord, the God of Israel, "I anointed you king over Israel, and I delivered you out of the hand of Saul; and I gave you your master's house."

It is obvious that the motif is parallel; but, beyond that, one can observe that it has the same function and stands in the same place as in the structure of the prophetic speech.

Though the speeches in the books of Kings have been integrated into the narrative and are certainly inexact, one may assume that behind them there is still a very old form

157

of the prophetic speech, and indeed, a very old form of prophecy (court prophecy) which was associated with kingship in a special way. In the copies of the judgment-speeches which are preserved for us, the motif of " the earlier saving acts of God to the King " suggests a relationship with the prophecy of Nathan (II Sam., ch. 7). This is the aspect of this prophecy that naturally recedes sharply from prominence in the accounts that have been preserved for us — the strengthening and confirmation of the kingship from the viewpoint of God (cf. I Kings 9:1-9).

This motif of contrast provides us with a noteworthy link between judgment prophecy and salvation prophecy. Against the background of this prophecy, the unconditional judgment prophecy of the writing prophets and a few of their predecessors stands out all the more sharply.

A conjecture about the form of the later two-part announcement of judgment might be ventured here. We have seen that the utterly simple one-part JI does not yet need to contain the " I of God," i.e., a speech in the first person (of God). We just saw that the motif, " the intervention of God," originates in salvation prophecy, thus in the intervention of God against Israel's enemies (or the king's enemies) (Isa. 37:29 f.). It is possible, then, that this kind of speech in which God speaks in the first person in the part of the announcement that tells of the intervention of God originated in salvation prophecy. We also know that there is ample evidence for this in the " handing over formula " of the holy war: " Behold, I give . . . into your hand." That such a transformation (intervention of God for his people — against his people) was possible is seen in the relation between Jer. 22:25 and Isa. 22:17 f.

(e) The Sign

The collation of all the judgment-speeches directed to an individual has produced the especially remarkable and important observation that the greater part of these speeches is connected with the announcement of a sign.

158

I Sam. 2:27-36: v. 34: And this . . . shall be the sign to you [Eli]: both of them [his sons] shall die on the same day.

I Sam. 15:10-31: v. 27: Saul laid hold upon the skirt of his robe, and it tore.

II Sam. 12:7b-14: v. 14: The child . . . shall die.

I Kings 11:29-40: vs. 30 f.: Then Ahijah laid hold of the new garment . . . , and tore it.

I Kings 13:1-3: v. 3: The altar shall be torn down.

I Kings 14:7-16: v. 12: When your feet enter the city, the child shall die.

Isa. 7:14: Therefore the Lord himself will give you a sign.

Isa. 37:30 f.: And this shall be the sign for you . . .

In this collection of texts one can see that there is a primary and essential union of word and sign in the prophetic speech. The later symbolic actions of the writing prophets are grounded in this primary union. *Always*, these signs are related to the announcement and never to its reason, the accusation. (But the accusation can also be associated with the parabolic speech: II Sam., ch. 12, and I Kings 20:38-40.) The reason that a sign is attached to the announcement in so many cases is that the thing announced will only appear later, perhaps after several years. Its intention, therefore, is to attest to the speech in the hour in which it was delivered. It is possible, and even probable, that the sign also belonged originally to the announcement of salvation (just as in Isa. 7:1-9; 37:30 f.) and passed from there into the announcement of judgment (as Isa. 7:10-17 shows). Later the sign was disconnected from the word and is very seldom joined to it in the writing prophets.

I Kings 21:19 shows how it was possible for the sign to become included in the speech, " In the place where dogs licked up the blood of Naboth." This sentence is not absolutely necessary for the announcement of judgment, as II Kings 1:6 shows. What the sentence contains beyond the

159

mere announcement is a sign: If the death of Ahab happens at a certain place . . . , then that *shows* the witnesses that the announcement of Elijah has come true. The only distinction is that the sign is postponed from the time the word is spoken to the time it comes true.

The whole complex of prophetic signs shall remain outside of consideration here. The evidence just given is sufficient to show that *essentially* they belong to the prophetic speech.

(f) The Correspondence of the Announcement and the Accusation

In the passage just named, I Kings 21:19, the sign that was incorporated into the speech contains a reference that relates the announcement to the previous accusation, the punishment to the guilt. The stating of the place at which the misfortune will overtake the king is enlarged by a relative sentence that refers to the transgression of the king (quite similar to Ezek. 17:16). This kind of allusion to a prior event is extraordinarily frequent in the later prophetic speeches. There are numerous possibilities for such allusions or references to the accusation in the announcement. It is also found often in the early form of the JI:

I Sam. 15:23: Because you have rejected the word of the Lord, he has also rejected you from being king.

II Sam. 12:7 ff.: You have smitten Uriah the Hittite with the sword, and have taken his wife to be your wife, . . .

10: Now therefore the sword shall never depart from your house, . . .

11: and I will take your wives before your eyes, and give them to your neighbor.

I Kings 20:42: Therefore your life shall go for his life.

I Sam. 2:29: Why then look with greedy eye at my sacrifices . . . ?

32: Then in distress you will look with envious eye on all the prosperity which shall be bestowed upon Israel.

160

II Kings 20:17: Behold, the days are coming, when all that is in your house . . . shall be carried to Babylon.

Especially telling is the passage, II Sam. 12:7 ff. It is also possible here as in the other passages that this correspondence only goes back to the style of the narrator. At least in I Kings 21:19, however, that is not probable due to the extremely strong form of the speech. It is more reasonable to assume that already in the earliest form of the prophetic speech, this reference or allusion brings out the corresponding relationship between transgression and punishment. These correspondences which run through the whole history of the prophetic judgment-speech seem to me to be a sure sign that each part of the judgment-speech is built upon the other and could not have separate roots.

I still cannot answer the question about the origin and meaning of this correspondence motif.

4. *Judgment-Speeches Without a Reason.* Within the announcement there is a small group that does not belong with the announcements of judgment but to an entirely different form, despite a deceptive similarity. It is the group of announcements that have *no* reason:

II Kings 20:1 (= Isa. 38:1) :
   Thus says the Lord,
   " Set your house in order;
   for you shall die, you shall not recover."

Jer. 22:10: Weep not for him . . .
   but weep bitterly for him who goes away,
   for he shall return no more
   to see his native land.

11 f.: For thus says the Lord concerning Shallum . . . :
   " He shall return here no more, but in the place where they have carried him captive, there shall he die, and he shall never see this land again."

161

22:24-27; 28 f.; 30: [Jehoiakim]
    24: As I live, says the Lord,
       though Coniah the son of Jehoiakim, king of
       Judah,
       were the signet ring on my right hand,
       yet I would tear you off
    25: and give you into the hand of those who . . . ,
       into the hand of those of whom . . . .
    26: I will hurl you and the mother . . . into an-
       other country . . .
       and there you shall die.
    28: [A complaint against Jehoiakim.]
    30: Thus says the Lord:
       "Write this man down as childless,
       a man who shall not succeed in his days;
       for none of his offspring shall succeed
       in sitting on the throne of David."
Jer. 37:17: [Zedekiah]
       " Is there any word from the Lord? "
       Jeremiah said, " There is."
       Then he said, " You shall be delivered into the
       hand of the king of Babylon."

In these six speeches death, or exile, or the like is announced to a king (Hezekiah, Shallum = Jehoahaz; Coniah = Jehoiakim; Zedekiah) without depicting this as
punishment for a transgression and without basing it on
an accusation. One can point out that both kings, Jehoahaz
and Jehoiakim, only ruled for three months; but that is
not sufficient since accusations in different speeches were
made against Zedekiah. The reason for the absence of an
accusation is seen in the speeches to Hezekiah and Zedekiah; they are answers to an inquiry by the king. In Jer.,
ch. 22, the speech does not deal with an inquiry from these
kings, but that does not exclude the possibility that these
speeches are answers to questions. An account of such an
inquiry is also found in II Kings, ch. 1. This story is an
example of how an announcement of judgment could
come in answer to an inquiry. It deals with the great com-
162

plex concerning the questioning of God in the older form of the oracle — and the later prophetic inquiry (cf. my leading article, *Kerygma und Dogma* 1, Qu., 1960, pp. 2–30). In many cases the answer had the form of an announcement (e.g., the questioning of an oracle in connection with holy war). This is, however, something essentially different from the prophetic announcement of judgment that is never determined by the inquiry of the addressee but by a transgression that he committed.

Here, an important distinction can be seen between the AS and the AJ: an announcement of salvation can certainly be an answer to a question as shown especially well by the sentence from the holy war, " Behold, I give into your hand." This is not possible in an announcement of judgment. The mere announcement of ill (*Unheilsankündigung*) which we find in this group of texts should be distinguished clearly from the announcement of judgment.

EXCURSUS: PROPHETIC SPEECHES IN THE BOOKS OF CHRONICLES

In I Chronicles only two prophetic speeches are found that are parallel to those in the books of Kings: I Chron. 17:1-4; II Sam., ch. 7; and I Chron. 21:9-17; II Sam., ch. 24; as well as in II Chron. 11:2-4; I Kings 12:21-24; II Chron., ch. 18; I Kings, ch. 22. There is a separate body of the prophetic speeches that are only found in II Chron. 12:5-8; 15:1-7; 16:7-10; 19:2-3; 20:14-18; 20:37; 21:12-15; 24:20; 25:7-8; 25:14-16.

Even if all these speeches are constructions of the Chronicler, a summary judgment about " authenticity " or " inauthenticity " is not methodologically permissible. One must inquire into the place held by each individual speech in the history of the prophetic speech.

(1) A few of these speeches have practically nothing in common with the original form of the prophetic judgment-speech and are no more than the form used to express the Chronicler's interpretation of history; II Chron. 12:5-8; 15:1-7; 16:7-10; 19:2-3; 21:12-15 (in part). In all of these, one can still find traces of the polarity of the original prophetic speech with its

163

two parts, but they have lost their sharpness in that now both parts are conditional:

> II Chron. 15:2: The Lord is with you, while you are with him.
> . . . but if you forsake him, he will forsake you.

But when once the accusation made was unconditional and therefore the announcement of judgment also seems at first to be unconditional, it is later attenuated:

> 12:5: You abandoned me, so I have abandoned you to the hand of Shishak.

But then it says:

> 6: Then the princes of Israel and the king humbled themselves.

and a new speech of God is now uttered:

> 7: They have humbled themselves; I will not destroy them.

Or in II Chron. 16:7-10 the prophetic speech is no longer an announcement but a later interpretation of two completed incidents — a victory and a defeat. The former happened " because you relied on the Lord." In II Chron. 21:12-15, in the " letter of Elijah " it is announced that a terrible plague is coming upon the people and the reason given for this is the godless behavior of the king, Jehoram: " Because you . . . have walked in the way of the kings of Israel, and have led Judah and the inhabitants of Jerusalem into unfaithfulness. . . ." In two prophetic speeches the reason given is a coalition of the Judean kings with northern Israel: chs. 19:2-3 and 20:27; in ch. 25:7-8 a prophet gives the king a corresponding instruction which he follows.

In all these speeches the prophets express the thesis of the Chronicler's view of history so plainly, one might even say so obviously, that one must at least reckon with a transformation by the Chronicler, but probably with his own construction.

(2) But this is not all that can be said for these prophetic speeches. Even if scarcely any of these speeches can be consid-

164

ered as a literal repetition of a prophetic speech exactly as it was spoken, they nevertheless indirectly contain a good, genuine prophetic tradition.

(a) In regard to ch. 20:14-18, G. von Rad has shown that "the promise of success in the holy war is preserved here in a manner astonishingly close to the very old speech forms from the holy war" (op. cit., pp. 80 f.).

(b) In a few prophetic speeches elements are preserved that clearly remind one of the JI. One of the two forms of the accusation which we found there was the accusing question in a personal address. It is found again in a few of the prophetic speeches of the Chronicler:

II Chron. 19:2: Should you help the wicked and love those who hate the Lord?
24:20: Why do you transgress the commandments of the Lord, so that you cannot prosper?
25:15: Why have you resorted to the gods of a people, which did not deliver their own people from your hand?

Here in v. 16 an announcement of judgment that belongs to it can still be seen:

16: I know that God has determined to destroy you, because you have done this and have not listened to my counsel.

The other form of the accusation in the form of a statement is perhaps also still recognizable in a few speeches:

II Chron. 16:9: You have done foolishly in this; for from now on you will have wars.
20:37: Because you have joined with Ahaziah, the Lord will destroy what you have made.
21:13b: And [because] also you have killed your brothers, of your father's house, who were better than yourself;
14: behold, the Lord will bring a great plague on your people, your children, your wives, and all your possessions,
15: and you yourself will have a severe sickness.

The astonishing thing now is that *all* of these speeches, with one exception (ch. 24:20), are actually prophetic speeches directed to the king! This shows that the unity of function and form of the JI has been preserved all the way down to the work of the Chronicler. This fact is much more important than an answer to the questions: What is genuine in each speech? What is modified by the Chronicler? What are his new constructions? This striking and indisputable unity of function and form in a considerable part of the prophetic speeches of the Chronicler offers a secure basis for assuming that there were prophets, not only (or almost only) in the Northern Kingdom during the period of the kingship, as it seems in the Deuteronomistic historical writings, but that they were also present all through the whole history of the kingship in the Southern Kingdom. It is no longer possible to know why Deuteronomistic historical work did not admit this prophetic tradition from the Southern Kingdom.

(c) A brief inspection of the history of the forms of these prophetic speeches still enables us to recognize a step in the history of its tradition. After what has just been said it is clear that the real interest of the Chronicler in including the prophetic speeches was to give divine authority to his interpretation of history derived from the Deuteronomistic interpretation. It would be grotesque to believe, however, that he might have simply invented for this purpose the names of the prophets, the events in which they appeared, and their words. Doubtless he had access to traditions telling of the appearance of these prophets. That can be gathered immediately from the form of two of these speeches; II Chron. 16:7-10 is a construction of the Chronicler in its present form. In v. 9, however, one can surmise that this was an older, very short form of the prophetic speech which could have been quite similar, though probably not literally identical, to a genuine speech of Hanani to the king, Asa. In II Chron. 21:12-15 the older and later form still stands out visibly; in vs. 12b-13a the accusation is general, abstract, and theologically formulated — reminiscent of a Deuteronomistic formulation. But in v. 13 a quite different, very concrete accusation (see above) is added. The announcement of judgment in vs. 14 f., which goes with it, has many features (punishment of the house of the king) that re-

166

mind one of a very old form, so that one can presume here that behind the Chronicler's work is an older, very short, and pregnant prophetic speech that is similar to the JI in the books of Kings and whose historicality is not questioned.

(d) Finally, there is one other important feature to be mentioned. It is reported in Chronicles with notable frequency that a prophet must suffer because of a judgment-speech opposing the king:

II Chron. 16:10: Then Asa was angry with the seer [Hanani], and put him in the stocks.

24:21 f.: But they conspired against him [Zechariah], and by command of the king they stoned him with stones in the court of the house of the Lord. . . . And when he was dying, he said, " May the Lord see and avenge! "

25:16: But as he [a prophet] was speaking the king said to him, "Have we made you a royal counselor? Stop! Why should you be put to death? "

In Chronicles, with its harmonizing and idealizing tendencies, this element is certainly very striking. In regard to II Chron. 16:10, Rudolph says that " the Chronicler needed to account for the severe sickness of Asa in his latter years from the viewpoint of his belief in retribution. Obviously the fate of Jeremiah has served as his prototype." That may be right, but if one takes the other passages into consideration as well, this explanation no longer suffices. In each of the three passages the suffering of the prophet is related in a different way and in ch. 24:21 f. it is told very vividly. Even if — and this is very improbable — in all three the suffering of the prophet should have furnished the reason each time for the ill that befell a king, it could not have been simply invented or *only* inferred from the fate of Jeremiah. On the contrary, it is a more likely assumption that this strong feature — the suffering of the prophets — which was caused by the anger of the king, was already at the disposal of the Chronicler in his prophetic traditions. This element is also found in the Deuteronomistic presentation and so there are no grounds here for maintaining

167

that it was an intervention. If, as we saw, the early form of these prophetic speeches in the Chronicles which still can be inferred from the later form was an *unconditional* announcement of judgment, one could *well* understand how the kings who were affected by these prophets would have wanted to silence them.

In any case, one can say that this element of the suffering of the prophets certainly was not suited to the Chronicler's transformation of the prophetic speeches in which the unconditional announcement of judgment is mostly deflected or attenuated. On the other hand, however, it is very well suited to the early form that is concealed behind them.

(3) Three old forms of prophetic speech can be identified within the speeches of Chronicles: (1) the promise of success from the holy war (II Chron. 20:14-18) ; (2) the prophetic instruction (probably in answer to a question of the king), II Chron. 11:2-4; II Kings 12:21-24; and II Chron. 25:7-8; (3) the JI which can still be recognized many times after the Chronicler's revision. In this transition the distinction was now no longer made between the JI and the JN and one also sees a complete dissolution of the old forms.

D. The Announcement of Judgment Against Israel (JN)

I. THE ANNOUNCEMENT OF JUDGMENT AGAINST ISRAEL AS A FURTHER DEVELOPMENT OF THE ANNOUNCEMENT OF JUDGMENT AGAINST THE INDIVIDUAL

It has often been said that the prophetic speech as it is found in the writing prophets from the time of Amos on, already represents a developed form, and is by no means the historical origin of a speech form.[1] At least a branch of this earlier history which must be assumed for the writing prophets is to be seen in the structure and history of the prophetic judgment-speech to the individual (JI) that is explained in the previous section.[2] This earlier history makes it possible for us to uncover a basic type of the prophetic judgment-speech in the judgment-speeches against Israel, which form the major component of the prophetic speeches in the writing prophets of the eighth and seventh centuries. This constitutes a further development of the JI. The single essential distinction is that these speeches are directed to the nation, Israel, or to organic groups within this nation, members of the body politic. In this change of the speech's address, the reason can be found for the subtle distinctions in the form. The lowness of the horizon in which the occurrence of the JI takes place makes possible a form with one part in the accusation as well as in the

169

announcement of judgment, thus enabling the entire speech to be short. In addition to that, the way the accusation and the announcement stand side by side without any verbal connection gives these speeches the thoroughly pre-literary character of speeches that were spoken in direct address.

It is through a change of the addressee that the horizon of the prophetic judgment-speech is broadened; since *the accusation* is directed to a majority, a " corporate personality," it usually includes a large number of transgressions. This makes it necessary for the accusation to be uttered sometime after the individual deed — the accusation can only be made when a number of these deeds have accumulated. That results in the division of the accusation into two parts [8]: the accusation that is made against the nation or a group names the transgression at the outset in a general conceptual form, and then it is developed by making it more concrete, exemplifying it, or giving a citation (Amos 2:1):

Accusation: For three transgressions of Moab, and for four . . . ;
Development: because he burned to lime the bones of the king of Edom.

With this collection of a series of offenses into one concept which again makes it necessary to concretize, a variation appears at the same time in the grammatical form: this accusation which is conceptually formed and then concretized is uttered in the third person; it is spoken no longer or at least less frequently in the second person of direct address.

The *announcement* in the JN is also divided into two parts. While in the accusation the length of time is greater between the concrete transgressions and the prophet's speech in which they are collected, in the announcement the length of time grows between the prophet's utterance expressing the verdict of God and the fulfillment of that
170

which is announced in it. Both of these poles can only be held together because it is God himself who executes that which is announced.[4] For that reason, the first part of the announcement now becomes the intervention of God in a speech by God in the first person; the second part, which corresponds to it, is the result of this intervention, namely the punishment spoken in the third person (Hos. 13:8), which is to befall the one addressed:

Intervention of God: I will fall upon them like a bear robbed of her cubs, I will tear open their breast,

Results of the Inter-
vention: and there I will devour them like a lion, as a wild beast would rend them.

Further examples are: Isa. 8:5-8; 9:7-11, 17-20; 22:8b-14; 28:7-13; 29:13-14; 30:12-14, 15-17.

Thus, on the basis of the changed addressee and the expansion that is associated with it, the explanation is given for the division of both parts of the JN into two sections. This does not provide the reason for the change in the messenger formula which joins the two parts. A certain alteration also precedes this connective member, but more about that later. There are still, however, a large number of JN's in which the messenger formula has the same wording, "therefore, thus says Yahweh" or abbreviated, "therefore," and stand in the same place, i.e., after the reason and before the announcement. Thus, the basic structure of the prophetic judgment-speech to the nation can be outlined as follows:

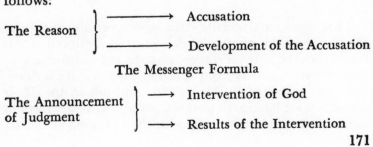

The Reason ⟶ Accusation
⟶ Development of the Accusation

The Messenger Formula

The Announcement of Judgment ⟶ Intervention of God
⟶ Results of the Intervention

Aside from the fact that the parts have two members, this structure agrees with the JI. Here, the introduction, which is often a summons to hear, is left out in order to show only the major lines.

Nevertheless, a qualification must be made immediately; we had said that in the JI we always have a *pre*literary form. It still is very similar to the elements of the regular judicial procedure out of which it has grown; this can be seen, above all, in the laconical brevity and pregnance of all the elements that we could, in one passage, compare directly with the forms of the apodictic law. With this form the texts containing the prophetic speeches correspond almost altogether to this one structure. There are few variants and hardly any expansions.

That is fundamentally different in the corpora of speeches that have come down from the writing prophets. *These speeches are completely literary formations.* The prophetic speeches first began to be passed down in a special tradition independent of the accounts, when the change took place in their addressee, so that the prophetic judgment-speech was now directed to the whole people. This resulted in the division of both parts of the speech — the accusation as well as the announcement. The fact that this speech which had only one member in the JI is later divided into two parts can be proved a hundredfold. Along with this, an alteration in the character of the prophetic announcement of judgment took place. It deviated noticeably from the event to which it originally belonged, and became in its unfettered state, a new and freer formation.

That becomes especially clear in one certain feature of the history of the prophetic speech; an inner development causes the relatively short speeches to be expanded into very long unities (such as from Amos to Ezekiel). This development first began in the JN only and not in the JI. It would not yet have been possible in the preliterary form of the JI, but could only begin with the changing of the ad-
172

dressee when there is a greater interval between the utterance of the speech and the effects.

This freer formation which is not bound so tightly to the structure of the JN can be seen from the beginning in all the writing prophets. This makes it still more evident that the tradition of the prophetic speeches which is present in these books must have already had a previous history. For this reason it is impossible to rediscover the structure that was shown above in each prophetic speech. It is much more prudent to note that this framework of the prophetic judgment-speech is fundamental only to the *genre* and that the expression of an individual speech can deviate very far from it. Because of this greater freedom, the basic structure of the prophetic judgment-speech, which remained the same from Amos to Ezekiel, does not hinder the formulation of the speech in personal language, the assimilation of different traditions, or the adaptation of the speech to the ever-changing situations of the different prophets of the eighth and seventh centuries. On the contrary, it is precisely the personal expression of the prophetic message that is the outstanding characteristic of this second epoch of prophecy, while the prophecy of the first period can be anonymous.

If this delimitation has been expressed clearly enough, then it can now be said that we are able to recognize a *basic form* of the prophetic judgment-speech to the nation which is fundamental to the most comprehensive genre of prophetic speech.[5] It runs through the whole history of prophecy from the point where the judgment-speech to the whole nation is first encountered to its complete dissolution.

These examples show that we are justified in speaking of a basic form of the judgment-speech to the nation; but, at the same time, they show that we are not dealing here with a rigid scheme. These few examples have already shown the freedom with which this form can be expressed. Among these some examples were selected that have the closest possible correspondence to the basic form; the most have a special and independent character through all kinds of

173

	Amos 4:1-2	Hos. 2:5-7	Isa. 8:6-8	Isa. 30:12-14	Micah 3:1-2, 4
Reason — Introduction	Hear this word, you cows of Bashan, who are in the mountain of Samaria,	—	—	—	Hear, you heads of Jacob and rulers of the house of Israel!
Accusation	who oppress the poor, who crush the needy,	For their mother has played the harlot; she that conceived them has acted shamefully.	Because this people have refused the waters of Shiloah that flow gently,	Because you despise this word, and trust in oppression and perverseness, and rely on them;	Is it not for you to know justice? — you who hate the good and love the evil,
Development	who say to their husbands, "Bring, that we may drink!"	For she said, "I will go after my lovers, who give me my bread and my water, my wool and my flax, my oil and my drink."	and melt in fear before Rezin and the son of Remaliah;	and trust in oppression and perverseness, and rely on them;	who tear the skin from off my people, and their flesh from off their bones;
Announcement — Messenger Formula	The Lord God has sworn by his holiness	Therefore	therefore, behold,	therefore	—
Intervention of God	that, behold, the days are coming upon you,	I will hedge up her way with thorns; and I will build a wall against her,	the Lord is bringing up against them the waters of the River, mighty and many, …	this iniquity shall be to you like a break in a high wall, bulging out, and about to collapse, whose crash comes suddenly, in an instant;	Then they will cry to the Lord, but he will not answer them; he will hide his face from them.
Results of the Intervention	when they shall take you away with hooks, even the last of you with fishhooks.	so that she cannot find her paths. She shall pursue her lovers, but not overtake them; and she shall seek them, but shall not find them.	and it will rise over all its channels and go over all its banks; and it will sweep on into Judah, it will overflow and pass on, reaching even to the neck.	and its breaking is like that of a potter's vessel which is smashed so ruthlessly that among …	—

	Micah 2:1-4	Micah 3:9-12	Jer. 5:10-14	Jer. 7:16-18, 20
Introduction	Woe	Hear this, you heads of the house of Jacob and rulers of the house of Israel,	"Go up through her vinerows and destroy; but make not a full end; strip away her branches, for they are not the Lord's.	As for you, do not pray for this people, or lift up cry or prayer for them, and do not intercede with me, for I do not hear you.
Accusation	to those who devise wickedness and work evil upon their beds! When the morning dawns, they perform it, because it is in the power of their hand.	who abhor justice and pervert all equity,	For the house of Israel and the house of Judah have been utterly faithless to me.... They have spoken falsely of the Lord, and have said, 'He will do nothing;	Do you not see what they are doing in the cities of Judah and in the streets of Jerusalem?
Development	They covet fields, and seize them; and houses, and take them away; they oppress a man and his house, a man and his inheritance.	who build Zion with blood and Jerusalem with wrong. ...yet they lean upon the Lord and say, "Is not the Lord in the midst of us? No evil shall come upon us."	no evil will come upon us, nor shall we see sword or famine. The prophets will become wind; the word is not in them....' "	The children gather wood, the fathers kindle fire, and the women knead dough, to make cakes for the queen of heaven; and they pour out drink offerings to other gods, to provoke me to anger.
Messenger Formula	Therefore thus says the Lord:	Therefore because of you	Therefore thus says the Lord, the God of hosts:	Therefore thus says the Lord God:
Intervention of God	Behold, against this family I am devising evil, from which you cannot remove your necks; and you shall not walk haughtily....	—	"Because they have spoken this word, behold, I am making my words in your mouth a fire, and this people wood, and the fire shall devour them."	Behold, my anger and my wrath will be poured out on this place, upon man and beast, upon the trees of the field and the fruit of the ground;
Results of the Intervention	In that day they shall take up a taunt song against you, and wail with bitter lamentation, and say, "We are utterly ruined; he changes the portion of my people; how he removes it from me! Among our captors he divides our fields."	Zion shall be plowed as a field; Jerusalem shall become a heap of ruins, and the mountain of the house a wooded height.	(The result of the intervention of God is anticipated in the introduction.)	it will burn and not be quenched.

Reason (Introduction–Development) · Announcement (Messenger Formula–Results of the Intervention)

variations of the basic form. The only thing remaining the same throughout all of these variations is that which constitutes the essence of the judgment-speech directed to Israel — the judgment of God is announced to the people because of specific failures. This establishes that it is determined by the accusation-announcement polarity and that the two parts themselves, most of which have two sections, are to be explained in terms of the above-mentioned distinction from the judgment-speech directed to the individual.[6]

The event itself, the utterance of the announcement of Yahweh's judgment to the people for a transgression, has therefore created the form; it contains nothing that might not be explained on the basis of this event. It is this complete adequacy of form which permits a multiplicity of variations. This shows the vitality of the prophetic speech.

The form-historical investigation of written prophecy should start with the definition and treatment of these variations, but this cannot be carried through to completion here. In concluding, however, a few examples should now be given that show how the basic form of the prophetic judgment-speech can still be recognized in a large number of modifications, expansions, and variant wordings.[6a]

II. MODIFICATIONS OF THE FORM

The sequence of both parts can be interchanged; therefore, the judgment-speech can begin with the announcement:

		Isa. 3:1-11	Amos 9:8-10	Jer. 2:26-28
Announce-ment	→ Intervention	1-4	8-9	26a
	→ Result	5-7	10a	26b

		Isa. 3:1-11	Amos 9:8-10	Jer. 2:26-28
Reason	⟶ Accusa- tion	(8a?) 8b	10a	27b
	⟶ Develop- ment	9a	10b	27a-28

(9b-11 Additions)

Further examples are: Isa. 7:18-25; 17:1-11; 17:12-14; 30:8-11; Hos. 9:7-9; 13:15 to 14:1; Jer. 13:25-27.

The sequence can also change within both of the parts; in Amos 5:12, 16, and 17, the results of the intervention of God in v. 17 are described in v. 16 (cf. also Isa. 28:14-22; Hos. 10:1-2).

In the example, Isa. 3:1-11, apart from the reversal of the sequence, the structure is not changed; one can see, nevertheless, a shifting of the emphasis. The announcement encompasses the greatest part of the speech, and the reason (vs. 8b-9a) diminishes in comparison with it. Obviously, the intention here is to shift the special emphasis to the announcement. The opposite can also occur. The announcement of judgment can be quite short or only implied, while all the rest of the speech is devoted to developing the reason. An example of this is Jer. 2:1-13; only v. 9 contains an announcement of judgment: " Therefore I still contend with you, says the Lord, and with your children's children I will contend "; all the rest of the speech gives the reason for the judgment announced in v. 9. But even where one of the parts is greatly diminished, the basic form is still present; that which is essential is not the external balance of emphasis nor the adherence to a pattern, but the correspondence of the judgment of God and the guilt of the people which is required by the proceedings.

This correspondence itself is still to be assumed, however, where the exterior connection between both of the parts has dissolved, and therefore, where the announcement

177

of judgment and the accusation are found separately. Here one might recall Balla's investigation of the Amos pericopies which started with the assumption that " reproach " and " threat " were independent units. He came to the conclusion that they are found far more frequently joined together than separated. This is close to the realization that the unity of both parts is the rule and that their separation is the exception. Then, however, the independent appearance of the " reproach " and the " threat " is not to be regarded as primary and their combination as secondary, as did Gunkel and many who followed him. On the contrary, it should be regarded as a secondary individuation of a single motif similar to that presumed by Gunkel in many Psalms such as the Psalms of Trust.[7] In the JI the parts of the judgment-speech are only very seldom — actually almost never — found separated from one another. When that happens much more frequently in the JN, the reason for it is again to be found in the difference of the addressee. The nearness of the word to the event in the JI requires that the accusation and verdict remain next to each other; on the other hand, in the greater distance of the word from the event in the JN, it is possible that the emphasis might fall entirely on one of the two parts and from that point, it is only a short step for one part to become completely independent.[8]

Isaiah 2:12-17 (intro. v. 10?) is only an announcement of judgment, but very clearly contains the accusation implicitly by calling into account (vs. 12b-16) all of the pride and loftiness which is the reason for the coming of the day of Yahweh; it is an accusation against arrogance that is typical of Isaiah. It is similar in Amos 3:13-15, where an announcement of judgment is implied by the accusation. As a matter of fact, both parts can even be recognized here — the general accusation is contained in v. 14a:

on the day I punish Israel for his transgressions . . .

and the concrete transgression can be recognized in the last words:

178

I will smite the winter house with the summer house;
and the houses of ivory shall perish,
and the great houses shall come to an end. . . .

Further examples are in Hos. 10:6b-8; 13:9-11.

Those which have only accusations are Hos. 5:1-2; 6:7-10; 7:1-7 (here the announcement is implied in vs. 2 f.) ; 12: 1-2; Jer. 2:20-25; 5:26-29, 30-31; 23:16-24.

Those which have only an announcement are Hos. 2:16-18, 21-23 (fragmentary?) ; 7:12-16 (fragmentary?) ; Jer. 13: 12-14, 18-19; 5:15-17; and in striking frequency Isa. 7:18-20, 21-22, 23-25. Here one cannot avoid noticing that three isolated announcements of judgment follow one another. A small collection seems to be present which is attached to v. 17 — the conclusion of ch. 7:1-17. It is designated by the introductory phrase " in that day " in vs. 18, 20, 21, 23. We know from other contexts that under certain circumstances only the announcement from a prophetic speech known in its entirety is passed down, i.e., cited. Thus it is in the speech of Micah (ch. 3:9-12) , which is cited in Jer. 26:18, and in the speech of Amos, which Amaziah cites in Amos 7:11. Also the word of God in the visions of Amos in chs. 7:7-9; 8:1-3; 9:1-4; and Jer. 1:11-15 is only an announcement. In all these places the presupposition is that the real word of God is the announcement; because of this, it can be passed down under certain circumstances without a reason.

With the loosening of the tight structure (in the JI and in the woe) in which the announcement always followed the accusation, the strong distinction is gradually lessened between the announcement as the real word of God and the reason that stands outside of the speech entrusted to the messenger. The messenger formula forfeits its pregnant meaning. Many times it is abbreviated to a mere " therefore"; this abbreviation is completely understandable because in the prophetic speeches to the people, there was no longer any interest in setting off the announcement, as the real word of God, from the reason. Now, it is no longer

179

a matter of a single transgression of an individual man which can be established by any witness, but a complex of sins, offenses, and disobediences which the authority of the word of God demanded be exposed. So, the messenger formula can now be abbreviated, reconstructed, or even left out entirely.

Where the sequence of the two parts is reversed, causing the speech to begin with the announcement, the messenger formula loses its function as a connection between both of the parts. In this case the reason is usually attached with " for," just as, in general, the causal-grammatical connection of both parts of the judgment-speech is now found very frequently.[9] One sees in this also the lessening of distinctions described above. The messenger formula completely loses its place in the speeches where the announcement has incorporated the accusation as Amos 3:13-15; Isa. 2:12-17.

As these distinctions are lessened the messenger formula appears frequently at the beginning of the speech, thereby designating the whole prophetic speech as the word of God. This happens relatively seldom in the prophecy of the eighth century, but frequently in Jeremiah, and all through Ezekiel. In contrast to the JI this is, above all, a portentous alteration of the prophetic speech. It can only be misunderstood when the message formula is considered to be in its original position when it comes at the beginning of the whole speech; this is the way it has been understood most of the time.

Finally, a modification becomes possible through the relaxation of the form. This modification is that one of the two parts occurs twice in the same speech. It appears only a few times in the prophecy of the eighth century, but frequently in Jeremiah, and is the rule in Ezekiel. It is already implied in Amos, chs. 1 and 2: the sentence that returns in each of the stanzas, " I will not revoke the punishment," already implicitly contains the announcement of judgment that appears one more time at the end of each stanza. In Micah 3:1-4 the accusation is taken up once again

180

in 4b; the reason is repeated in Jer. 5:7-11. Other passages similar to this are: Hos. 13:9-11; 5:8-14; 8:1-3; Isa. 17:1-11. A further relaxation of the form can be seen in the kind of sequential contrast in Hos. 4:4-10:

> . . . because you have rejected knowledge,
> I reject you from being a priest to me.
> And since you have forgotten the law of your God,
> I will also forget your children.

In the Deuteronomistic version of the speeches of Jeremiah, the manifold repetition is an outgrowth of the broad prose style; e.g., in the temple speech the reason, which had earlier been extensively developed, is summarized once more in the beginning of the announcement (v. 13):

> Jer. 7:13 f.: And now, because you have done all these things, says the Lord, and . . . you did not listen, . . . therefore I will . . .

III. EXPANSIONS

With the relaxation of the structure of the old speech form, a large number of expansions became possible. Such expansions are seldom encountered in the JI and then only in a rudimentary way; a sure sign that it represents the older form. It is in correspondence with this when the expansions of the JN in the prophecy of the eighth century still remain within limits, while they so proliferate in Jeremiah and then even more in Ezekiel, that the original speech form can hardly be recognized among the expansions.

Still the expansions, as such, can, under no circumstances, be considered as secondary; on the contrary, in the prophets of the eighth century especially, these expansions which do

181

not immediately belong to the structure of the judgment-speech often contain the most distinctive compositions of the individual prophets. All sentences in the speeches of Isaiah which say something about faith are such expansions!

1. *Expansions of the Accusation.* (a) The accusation is given against the background of the earlier saving acts of God. Amos 2:6-16 can serve as an exemplary model, for here in the series in chs. 1 and 2 the speech to Israel is the only one that has this expansion.

6a	Accusation:	For three transgressions of Israel . . .
6b-8	Development:	because they sell the righteous . . .
9-11	Expansion:	Yet I destroyed the Amorite before them. . . .
		Also I brought you up out of the land of Egypt.

This is generally the most important and most frequent expansion of the JN and it is found in all the writing prophets from Amos to Ezekiel: Hos. 9:10-13 and ch. 11, in each stanza; Isa. 5:1-7; Jer. 2:1-13; Micah 6:1-4; and it stands behind the heavier, more baroque expansion in Ezek., chs. 16 and 20. It is the only expansion that is already found in the early form of the JI as a reminder of the saving acts that God had manifested to the king.

In Amos 2:6-16, vs. 9 ff. show the foundation of the historical tradition on which judgment prophecy rested. Verses 9 f. correspond to the basic confession of Israel. A messenger's speech can therefore be expanded with a reference to the deeds of God. In the freedom of such expansion, however, the prophet remained bound to the tradition which had been given to him.

How a kind of prophetic historical description developed from this contrast motif can be seen in the development going from Amos, ch. 2, through Hos., chs. 9 to 11, Jeremiah (esp. ch. 2), and Ezekiel to the Deuteronomistic critique of history. A beautiful example of the transition is Hos. 10:1-2, in which the form of the JN is still recognizable in all its parts, but which at the same time, seems almost like a critical view of history.

1a Prior history: Israel is a luxuriant vine . . . .
1b,c Development of the accusation by a contrast: The more
. . .
2a Accusation: The heart is false.
 Results for Israel: now they must bear their guilt.
2b Intervention of God: The Lord will break down their altars.

It is similar in ch. 13:5-8, but the structure of the JN here is clearer. The small collection of speeches clearly set off in Hos. 9:10 to 13:11, in which each prophetic speech contains this expansion and which was obviously compiled on the basis of this criterion, shows that the contrast construction as an expansion of the JN was already recognized by those who transmitted the prophetic books.

This motif shows an inner development. At the first it is an expansion containing only a contrast: God's kind deed in the past is contrasted to the offense of the addressee (this is also seen in the Mari letters, letter 1; II Sam., ch. 12, and Hos. 11:1-4). A further step can already be seen, however, in Amos, ch. 2; joined to the kind deed of God is Israel's reaction to it in the past:

Amos 2:12: But you made the Nazirites drink wine, and commanded the prophets . . .

This is also the case in Hos. 10:1b; 11:2; Isa. 5:1-7; Jer. 2:1-9; and in the last stage of development in Ezek., chs. 16; 20; 23; where the negative reaction of Israel predominates.[10]

(b) The same contrast motif is found in still another form. In Amos 4:6-11 the saving action of God toward Israel in the past is not pictured as saving deeds, but rather, as devastating blows that should have warned Israel. Israel, however, did not pay any attention to all of these warnings

183

(Jer. 2:30; 3:3; 5:3). This obduracy motif is also encountered at other times in a different form; of particular note is Isaiah where it is pictured as a placing of oneself on self-made security, e.g., chs. 7:9; 28:15; or

Micah 3:11b: Yet they lean upon the Lord and say,
"Is not the Lord in the midst of us? No evil shall come upon us."

This motif is encountered as an expansion of the accusation. It can be extended still farther when the prophet reprimands the ones addressed by pointing out the true relationship that is demanded of them.

Isa. 5:12: but they do not regard the deeds of the Lord, or see the work of his hands
31:1: but do not look to the Holy One of Israel
Amos 6:6: but are not grieved over the ruin of Joseph!
(cf. Jer. 8:11 f.)

(c) It is only a small step from such reprimanding to a reproach or warning such as in Amos, ch. 5:

6: Seek the Lord . . . , v. 14: Seek good . . . , v. 15: establish justice in the gate . . . .

Or in Isa. 1:17: "learn to do good; seek justice" (chs. 28: 12; 31:3); or the warning in Isa. 28:12, 22; the warning is found in v. 22, where the announcement is divided into judgment and salvation. Even if they are borrowed speech forms, these imperatives can still be explained as a development that grew out of the prophetic judgment-speech itself. This is shown by Jer. 2:19 and 2:25a.

The reproach and warning are certainly not genuine prophetic speech forms, but probably originate in the paranesis of the commandment as it can already be found in its early stage in the book of the covenant and in a developed form in Deuteronomy. In its origin it then was related to the speech by God which delivers a command and its

184

paranetic extension. On the basis of the Mari letters one can assume that in Israel the reproach could have also been taken over from salvation prophecy into judgment prophecy. *That* this form was taken over, however, is due to the judgment-speech itself as the remonstrances in its expansions show.

(d) In Hos. 9:7-9 is found the expansion of the accusation:

> The prophet is the watchman of Ephraim . . .

Up until that point the sentence is only an expansion of the accusation which makes it concrete. But then it goes farther:

> Yet a fowler's snare is on all his ways, and hatred in the house of his God.

" Fowler's snare " is a typical figure of speech in the lament of the individual over the persecution of the pious by the transgressor. In this sentence from the accusation raised against the people, one can clearly perceive how the first traces of the lament of the prophet appear. In Jeremiah we find it again enlarged into a whole poem of lamentation. The protestation of innocence belongs to this as an important motif; it was also implied by Hosea in ch. 3:5-8 (against the false prophets) in the expansion in v. 8: " But I am."

(e) An expansion of the accusation that is characteristic of the prophet Jeremiah is contained in the two speeches Jer. 5:1-6 and 6:27-30: it is determined by the question of whether the accusation actually concerns everyone. In order to make this clear Jeremiah receives the commission to verify it (to reinvestigate and to assay) ; in both places the expansion comes out with the answer that the accusation does indeed concern all.

(f) In this same direction is the prohibition of intercession in Jer. 7:16; 11:14; 14:11 f.; and Hos. 6:1-6. It is implied in the visions of Amos in chs. 7 to 9. Probably one

185

cannot speak of an expansion of the accusation in this motif since it is too independent. In the passages where the announcement of judgment follows the lamentation of the people rather than the expected salvation-speech, the disjunction of judgment prophecy and salvation prophecy can be recognized.

2. *Expansions of the Announcement.* (a) In Isa. 10:28-32 the announcement of judgment is predominated by a new motif — the dramatic description of the approach of the enemy. It does not belong necessarily to the announcement of judgment and was not a part of it in the beginning. It is never found in Amos, Hosea, and Micah; it is found only in Isaiah (chs. 5:26-30; 10:28-32) in the eighth century; and in Jeremiah in the so-called Scythian songs (chs. 4:5-29; 6:1-8, 22-26). This motif of the approach of the enemy has found its most beautiful, poetic expression in Jer., ch. 4. Here it approximates the prophetic judgment-speech so closely that both of its parts clearly stand out. The poem as a whole is an announcement of judgment; it contains as its reason the accusation (v. 17b) and its expansion (v. 18). In both of the passages in Isaiah the motif is still completely independent. Certainly, there is an independent motif here that was originally foreign to prophecy. Its origin is still unclear. Later it has probably been extended into a description of annihilation perhaps like Nahum 2:2-4, and lives on still later in the apocalyptic descriptions of the end.[10a]

(b) A completely different expansion of the judgment-speech can be seen in a series of passages in Isaiah, each of which deal with the intervention of God. This is not simply an intervention that brings judgment; a way is also opened for the protecting and redeeming action of God. This expansion can be seen the most clearly in chs. 7:1-9, 10-17, and 28:14-22. Ahaz's unbelief (ch. 7:10-13) causes a division to occur within the announcement: the judgment-speech is intended for the king (v. 17); along with that,

186

however, the salvation-speech remains (vs. 14-16) , but now it is only intended for those who believe (v. 9) . In ch. 28:14-22, the judgment-speech (vs. 17b-22) is directed to the " scoffers " (v. 14) ; but in the middle of the destruction, God lays the cornerstone of a new Zion in which only those who believe will participate (v. 16b) . A sign is given with this both times; this corresponds completely to the function of the sign in the earlier prophetic speeches. This lends support to conjecture that the sign originally belonged to the salvation-speech. Similar expansions, which point beyond judgment, are found in Isaiah in ch. 1:21-28 (the sentences 25b, 26) ; in ch. 1:18-20, v. 20; in ch. 30:15-17, v. 15; in ch. 28:7-13, v. 12. This shows that all sentences about believing in Isaiah (or synonymous) are found in this, an expansion! This makes it possible to determine the place and function of the concept of faith in Isaiah more clearly than has been possible before.

3. *Expansions of the Framework.* (a) The framework of the prophetic judgment-speech (introduction, transition, connecting formulas, and concluding formulas) in the early part of its history is either not present at all or only very sparingly (the messenger formula did not originally belong to the framework; it is a component of the prophetic speech) . From Jeremiah on it grows by leaps and bounds. A great number of introductory, transition, and concluding formulas are present for the first time in his speeches.[11] In Ezekiel the words and sentences that constitute the framework are even more abundant, and in Haggai and Zechariah they are excessively numerous. On the other hand, in Malachi they have practically disappeared.

The growth of the framework — probably the most certain sign of a historical development of the prophetic speech — means an increase in the sentences that identify the word of the prophet as God's word. It also seems certain to me that this growth means that in the course of its history the prophet's speech ceased being self-evident and self-under-

187

standable. The legitimation of the prophetic word as God's word became more and more necessary and thus the words of legitimation in the framework cumulated. In this growth of the framework which supported and legitimated the prophetic word there is evidence of the approaching end of prophecy.

(b) Three stages can be clearly distinguished in the history of the messenger formula. In the early period only the announcement is expressly designated as the word of God delivered by the messenger. Then, in a few speeches starting in the time of Amos, the messenger formula moves back to the beginning so that the whole speech, including the accusation, is designated as the word of God. Gradually this position of the messenger formula predominated, so that it now appears plainly as the introduction to the whole prophetic speech. Finally the formula becomes so rigid that it also is used to introduce speeches that make no claim to be messenger's speeches.[12] This means that the specific and original meaning of the messenger formula is lost.

The formula " It was the word of Yahweh to . . ." is found only from Jeremiah on. It is characteristic of the second epoch of prophecy in which the previously self-evident truth — that the prophetic word came forth from Yahweh — must be expressly stated in a regularly recurring introductory sentence.

(c) The so-called middle and end formula, $n^{e'}um\ yhwh$, does not belong to the prophetic speech but to that of the seer with respect to its origin; its original and characteristic usage is seen in Num. 24:3:

> The oracle of Balaam the son of Beor,
> the oracle of the man whose eye is opened. (Cf. II Sam. 23:1.)

After the office of seer had ceased to exist, prophecy adopted this old designation of the seer's speech; the position of the words offers certain proof of that. In the seer's speech, $n^{a}um$ in connection with the name of the seer introduces the speech, whereas in the prophetic speech where

188

this place was filled by the messenger formula, it could only occupy the place of an end or middle formula.[13]

It is difficult to say whether *nᵉum yhwh*, which is found frequently in Amos, belongs to the oldest version of the speech. In any case it is uncertain and could go back to the Judaistic redaction of the speeches of Amos. It is remarkable, however, that it is entirely missing in Hosea and is also used very seldom in Isaiah. It occurs often only in Jeremiah and Ezekiel. In any case, it does not belong to the genuine language of the messenger's speech (never in the JI). Certain proof can be offered for its origin in the seer's oracle.[14]

IV. VARIANTS OF THE PROPHETIC JUDGMENT–SPEECH

In a great many expansions of the JN indicated in the first section, it was shown how much we are dealing here with a free-floating form that can be developed in a number of different ways. It is not these many expansions as such that are noteworthy, however, but rather, the fact that the form remains stable with such a great possibility of variation. That is true to an even greater extent for the group of prophetic speeches that are enclosed in a different literary form and yet still belong to the genre of the prophetic judgment-speech. Gunkel was the first to show on a large scale that the prophets had borrowed other speech forms with which to enclose their message. Still more borrowed forms were then discovered in Old Testament prophecy by later investigators.

One can well utilize the concept of borrowing here, but even this does not describe the actual situation exactly enough. One must always ask: (*a*) what it is about each of the borrowed forms corresponding to the prophetic judg-

189

ment-speech that makes it suitable for borrowing, (*b*) whether and how the foreign speech form was assimilated by the prophetic judgment-speech, connected to it, or fused together with it, (*c*) whether perhaps through the borrowing of these forms which were foreign to the prophetic speech the speech itself was modified or developed in another direction. To make it clear from the beginning, one must ask whether, e.g., the use of the Priestly salvation-oracle and many psalm forms in Deutero-Isaiah is a basically and essentially different event than, e.g., the use of the parable form in Isa. 5:1-7 or the lament in Amos 5:1-2. The use of this form in Deutero-Isaiah shows, namely, that prophecy itself has become something essentially different. In Isaiah or Amos the use of the foreign forms did not change their message at all. Approximately in the middle between both stands Ezekiel where the clear adoption of Priestly speech forms did not bring with it a fundamental change in his message but only a relative modification.[15]

THE CRY OF WOE

The cry of woe stands out from the other variants as by far the most important and most frequent form. One might also be able to speak of a parallel formation of the JN. The woes (*Wehe-Worte*) form an especially tightly unified group of prophetic speeches, not only because of the introductory *hôy* which is the same in all of them, but also because of the same sequence of the two parts. *Hôy* always introduces the accusation, after which the announcement then follows. In this and in many other respects, the woe approximates the JI very closely. It deviates from the usual form at the outset, in that the introductory " woe! " itself represents something like an announcement of ill in *nuce*. One could imagine a prior form in which the " woe " was accompanied only by a reference to the one accused. This might remind one of certain curse formulas, and should

190

such a prior form have existed it would have to be understood as a prophetic variation of the curse. There are a few traces of the connection between curse and prophetic judgment-speech that still have to be investigated in more detail.

The woes are found predominantly in series: Isa., chs. 5; 28:1 to 33:1; Hab., ch. 2; perhaps also in Amos 5:18 and 6:1 (fragmentary?).[16] Again, that could correspond to the series of curses (Deut. 27:15-26). In addition to that, the series of woes in Hab., ch. 2, is spoken not against the Israelites but against the foreign conquerors, and is therefore related to salvation prophecy. The question is how the woe in salvation prophecy is related to that in judgment prophecy.

1. The Statistics and Form of the Woe. The word " *hôy*," which introduces the woe, is found in the Old Testament 50 times (plus 4 more with *kî*). It is completely restricted to the prophetic books (other than in I Kings 13:30, in a lament over death). Apart from two groups in which *hôy* has a different meaning (lament over death 7 times, a summons 9 times), all the expressions of woe belong to the form of the prophetic cry of woe. It is found 36 (plus 2?) times — 25 times against Israel and 11 times against foreign nations. For the most part they stand in series: 6(7) speeches in Isa., ch. 5 (also ch. 10:1), 6 (7) in Isa., chs. 28 to 31; 5 in Hab., ch. 2. Otherwise two or three occur together. We can assume that the series was a characteristic of the original form of the woe.

The introductory *hôy* is connected mostly with a participle (many times with an adjective) that determines the one to whom the woe is addressed (" woe to those who join house to house "). The woe followed by a participle is by nature concerned with a section of the whole and this section is defined by the participle. For this reason, the woe never refers to the whole nation and seldom does it refer to existing members of the group such as priests, prophets,

191

and the like. The woe is meant for those who have just done something specific. This makes the woe stand relatively close to the JI in which a specific deed is always presented. A special function of the woe can thus be seen here.

A striking feature is that the messenger formula is missing in most cases. In Isa., chs. 28 to 31, a transition between accusation and announcement is missing from all 7 woes. The same is true of the 6 woes in Hab., ch. 2, as well as in all of the woes against foreign nations. The messenger formula occurs regularly with " therefore " only in Jeremiah and Ezekiel, and thus only in the prophets of the seventh and sixth centuries. For this reason it can be safely assumed that the messenger formula originally had no place in the woe. It therefore was not a messenger's speech at first, but has been made to resemble one secondarily.

2. *The Announcement.* In the woes in Isa., ch. 5, Amos, chs. 5 f., and Heb., ch. 2, the announcement has one part, i.e., only the coming doom is announced and not an intervention of God (in the first person) . In the other passages it is quite different. In Isa., ch. 5, the insecurity of the relation of the accusation and announcement in the transmission of the text is striking. A series of woes is either passed down without an announcement, or the impression is given that the announcement was secondarily attached (Micah 2:1-3) , or there is a smooth transition between the two as in Hab., ch. 2. These observations indicate that the resemblance between the woe and the prophetic judgment-speech is only secondary.

3. *The Accusation.* (*a*) In Isa., ch. 5 (also Amos 5:7 ff.; Micah 2:1-3; Jer. 22:13-19) , the accusation in all the woes has a remarkably stable form. A *hôy* introduces a participial sentence that addresses the woe to the one doing the evil. A second closely parallel (synonymous) participial sentence is joined to it; following this is an explanatory sentence with a finite verb:

192

Woe to those who join house to house,
    who add field to field,
until there is no more room,
    and you are made to dwell alone
in the midst of the land.

The explicative second part of the accusation does not exhibit the same strength of style, and the relationship of the second part to the first is not always the same. One receives the impression that the first part — the actual cry of woe — has a very stable structure, whereas in the second part a greater freedom prevails. In addition to that, all these woes deal with a social accusation. Again the question arises of whether these might be related to the curses, since they are remarkably similar even with respect to style:

Cursed be he who slays his neighbor in secret. (Deut. 27:24.)
Woe to those who draw iniquity with cords of falsehood. (Isa. 5:18 f.)

The curses in Deut., ch. 27, are also concerned exclusively with the common life of the community. Here, moreover, some significance must be given to the fact that most of the woes like the curses were passed down in series. In any case it can be assumed that the group of woes in the writing prophets, just described, represents the original structure.

(b) A few additional forms can be recognized: In Isa. 30:1, 6 f., 2-5; 31:1-3 (perhaps ch. 29:15) the woe-speech is used in a special situation. In all three speeches Isaiah objects to the covenant with the Egyptians. Because of this situation the accusation becomes more complicated and these woes are given a strucure that deviates from the fixed form. Within the woes another group can be recognized which is concerned with the bad shepherd (s) : Jer. 23:1-4; Ezek. 34:1-16; Zech. 11:17. In Jeremiah and Ezekiel the form is largely dissolved. Zechariah 11:17 is most striking; it comes very close to being a curse-speech:

Woe to my worthless shepherd, who deserts the flock!
May the sword smite his right arm   and his right eye!
Let his arm be wholly withered,   his right eye utterly
                                      blinded!

Has the ancient curse form again come to the surface here in a later time when the prophetic speech forms were dissolved?

4. Woes Against the Enemies of Israel. The most stable group of woes other than in Isa., ch. 5, is the 6 (7) woes in Hab., ch. 2 (in addition Nahum 3:1-7; Isa. 33:1). Here in the first part is found the same strong synonymous parallelism consisting of participles introduced by *hôy*. It is different, however, in that the woe in all the speeches refers to one and the same conqueror who is not specified at the first by the participle connected by *hôy*. It is the same, in that the woe in all the speeches is limited to a specific sphere of action. There is something corresponding to this group in the curses, namely, the curses against enemy groups or peoples as Judg. 5:23; Gen. 49:5-7; 9:25. There is a very old woe against a foreign nation found in Num. 21:29 that is taken up again in Jer. 48:46 (text uncertain). Perhaps one can see here a transition from the curse to the woe. The woe against foreign nations could then have had a previous history in the early salvation prophecy.

EXCURSUS: THE CURSE AND THE ANNOUNCEMENT
OF JUDGMENT

There are many features and correlations that lead one to the conclusion that connections exist between the curse and the announcement of judgment. The most important complex that shows such contact is the Balaam story in Num., chs. 22 to 24. Balaam is a seer; as such he does not belong directly to the early history of prophecy. An indirect relation, however, certainly exists; the office of seer has grown into that of the prophet (I Sam. 9:9). The commission of the Moabite king to Balaam is: " Come now, curse this people for me " (Num. 22:6). The meaning of the insertion of the Balaam story into

194

the Yahwist's account of the occupation of the land is clear. The power of the curse and the blessing is, in itself, nonhistorical, and is like a kind of magic power that can be made effective in any way desired by the one who possesses it. In the Balaam story this power is made to serve the will of God and thus also the action of God toward Israel. This story proclaims that Yahweh alone is the lord of the blessing and the curse. From a theological viewpoint it is thus a parallel to Gen. 12:1-3, where the blessing and curse (the emphasis here lies completely on the blessing) are included and subordinated to the historical acts of Yahweh. In this event the basis is given for the transition from the curse to the judgment-speech. But now the Balaam story shows just as well as Gen. 12:1-3 that the emphasis always lies on the relationship of blessing to the historical actions of God. Balaam is called to curse, but under the direction of Yahweh's powerful command he must bless. In Gen. 12:1-3, Abraham receives a promise of blessing. In the course of further development one can see that the blessing is frequently and in diverse ways joined to the acting of God. God simply becomes the subject of the blessing. That is not always the case with the curse. Out of the 36 passages in which *'ārûr* is found, only 2 (Josh. 6:26 and I Sam. 26:19 — both Deuteronomic) contain the name of God. The curse therefore contains a pre- and extra-Yahwistic meaning — " Effective power, which does not require gods or spirits to make it effective." [17] The formulation, which is literally the same in Num. 24:9 and Gen. 12:3, shows this. The speech forms show the same things. While the curse largely remains bound to the curse formula *'ārûr*, the finite verb with God as its subject appears in the blessing in place of the participial formulation. This different development of the blessing and the curse provides the reason for the very early appearance of the judgment-speech in the place of the curse. There are a number of traces of this transition which can be detected.

A variation here is especially significant. Balaak, the king, gives the reason for his commission to Balaam to curse that nation by saying, " Since they are too mighty for me." Here the curse is a weapon that is employed against an enemy only in connection with a power struggle. The curse requires no other reason than the mere presence of opponents. It is note-

195

worthy now that, except for this passage, a reason is always given with the curse. This causes it to lose its magical character; it is found only with reference to the behavior of the one on whom the curse should fall. This can certainly be just as effective when directed to an individual as to a community.

The transition from the curse to the announcement of judgment can already be seen in one of the tribal aphorisms in Gen. 49:5-7 [17a]:

> 5: Simon and Levi are brothers;
>   weapons of violence are their swords.
> 6b: . . . for in their anger they slay men,
>   and in their wantonness they hamstring oxen.
> 7a: Cursed be their anger, for it is fierce;
>   and their wrath, for it is cruel!
> 7b: I will divide them in Jacob
>   and scatter them in Israel.

The present form of the saying was only possible after Israel came into existence. In this later form it represents the transformation of an earlier curse. Genesis 9:25 can serve as an example of this:

> Cursed be Canaan;
>   a slave of slaves shall he be to his brothers.

The curse consists of: (a) the curse ('ārûr with the calling of the name), (b) concretizing of the curse. It is completed by the addition of a reason for the curse, which is given here only in the narrative (in complete correspondence to this are the curses in Gen., ch. 3; Josh. 9:23). So a previous form can be assumed for Gen. 49:5-7 which might have sounded like this:

> Simon and Levi — be cursed!
> (For in their anger they slay men, and in their wantonness they hamstring oxen.)
> I will divide them in Jacob
>   and scatter them in Israel.

(Here the " in Jacob " and " in Israel " is probably also secondary.) In the present form both parts have been modified along the lines of the prophetic judgment-speech. The first part now consists of a concisely defined accusation, " Weap-

196

ons of violence are their swords," which is expanded in the second verse. The announcement of the intervention of God (Yahweh speaks in the first person!) with a modified curse is extraneously joined to this. As often happens, the curse is deflected because the direct cursing of a man is avoided.

It is certainly possible that this transformation of an old curse-saying [18] was undertaken first in the prophetic era; that is, however, improbable in ch. 49 which is otherwise very old. It is more probable to assume that this is a transition form between the curse and the judgment-speech. It became possible because in Israel the nonhistorical power of the curse was subjugated to God making it also necessary at the same time to give a reason for the curse. Genesis 4:5-7 is also such a transition form. The connection of the curse with a reason is seen especially well in the series of curses in the apodictic law (Deut. 27:15-26) ; all of these are curses which are only to take effect under certain circumstances (*Eventualflüche*) :

" Cursed be he who misleads a blind man on the road."

In all the passages the curse takes the place of the death punishment. Most of the transgressions named in the series are those which could be committed clandestinely and thus go unpunished.[19] In this case, the curse that has already been uttered and is still valid should take effect. A similar thing is true of the woes of the prophets of the eighth century which also appear in series. The deed with which these speeches are concerned would go unpunished without the prophetic judgment-speeches. The great propinquity of the series of curses in Deut., ch. 27, to the offenses in Ex. 21:12, 15-17 . . . (cf. Alt, *op. cit.*) , which are punishable with death, shows that the curse is already firmly joined to the legal procedure. It has lost its impersonal magical character. In the JI we found an amazing propinquity to the apodictic law. Since now the cursing of the perpetrator must take place in the cases where the deed would otherwise go unpunished, the propinquity of the cursing of the offender to the prophetic woe is completely understandable. Alt said concerning this: " That which was decisive for the actualization of this curse in a given case had therefore, to be done by Yahweh " (*op. cit.*, p. 314). He further distinguishes between the two series: " The one dealt with of-

197

fenses accessible to human prosecution and the other transgressions against Yahweh's basic demands which were reserved for divine requital" (p. 314). This makes it probable that not only the form but also the content of the prophetic woe originated with the curse, which was itself a part of legal practice.

A great many features of the curse, or of the speech forms that originally belonged to the curse, can be found in the prophetic announcement of judgment (not only in the woes). To mention only one example: In a Babylonian document a curse is uttered concerning the one who breaks the treaty and it terminates with the words, " He shall not return to his land." [19a] Exactly the same words are found in the speech of Jeremiah about Jehoiakim in Jer. 22:27. The statement encountered more frequently in the prophetic speeches, " God may make you like . . ." certainly has its origin in the curse.

How does this probable origin of the woe in the curse (i.e., in the curse already included in the Yahwistic law) relate to the prophetic speech as the speech of a messenger? It means that the woe is not a genuine prophetic speech genre. From the viewpoint of its origin it does not belong to the messenger's speech but to the borrowed speech forms that were inserted into or made to resemble the messenger's speech. Still there is an especial affinity between the woe and the announcement of judgment because the curse, which is included in the legal procedure (Deut., ch. 27), presupposed the future intervention of Yahweh against the offender exactly as did the prophetic woe.

It is possible that there was a previous history of the woe in salvation prophecy in which the woe was directed against Israel's enemies; Num., chs. 22 to 24, and the tribal aphorisms especially suggest this possibility. The evidence, however, is not adequate enough to allow a reconstruction of this earlier history.

All the questions of the relationship of the curse to the prophetic judgment-speech have not been thoroughly explained by what has been said. A comprehensive form-historical investigation of the curses recorded in the Old Testament and their background in other ancient religions has not yet been made.

198

V. VARIANT FORMULATIONS OF THE PROPHETIC SPEECH (BORROWED SPEECH FORMS)

The only variant formulations of the prophetic speech that will be treated here are those in which the speech is placed in a borrowed form such as that of a legal dispute. Single motifs and speech forms out of other areas which form only a component of the prophetic speech such as the provocation formula " Behold, I will . . ." will not be considered.[20]

1. *The Legal Procedure.* Texts: Isa. 1:18-20; 3:13-15; (5:1-7) ; Micah 6:1-5; Hos. 2:4-17, " Legal Procedure for Matrimonial Unfaithfulness " (cf. H. W. Wolff's commentary on this passage; 4:1-3, 4-6; 5:3-15; also noted that Jer. 2:5 ff.; 25:31 (nations) ; Mal. 3:5.

The legal procedure is the variant formulation that corresponds the closest to the prophetic judgment-speech. Indeed, it is nothing other than a dramatic description of what happened in every other JN but was just not depicted in these words. While in the usual JN the messenger speaks, in the legal procedure, God speaks as the judge directly and without any introduction (by a messenger formula) .

In Hos. 4:1-3 [21] the reason given for the summons to hear is, " for God holds court with the inhabitants of the land." The corpus of the speech (1b-3) which follows this introduction is a regular JN. The same is true of ch. 5:3-15, which is introduced by the same sentence. The judgment procedure, therefore, appears here in what the prophetic judgment-speech portrays. Outside of the introductory sentence one does not encounter any other single feature of the court procedure. It is similar in Hos. 4:4-6; 2:4-17. The judicial procedure comes through even less plainly in Jer. 2:5-29, where in v. 9, " contend " more nearly means the judging intervention of God against Israel, and in v. 5 the question that is characteristic of the judicial hearing (*Verhörfrage*) is only a rhetorical form. On the other hand, in the short speeches in Isa. 1:18-20 and 3:13-15 one can see the judicial procedure very clearly. Both are introduced with a summons to the court proceedings (as Isa. 43:20), then the complainant presents his case. In ch. 3:13-15 that happens in a direct accusation that is divided into metaphor and actuality. In ch. 1:18-20 the accusation is confronted with the assertion of the accused — that they are innocent. Both are in the form of a metaphor. Here the confrontation of the parties before the court can be seen very clearly. Following this in ch. 3:13-15 comes the question about the legal basis. This allows the accusation to be developed further. With this the speech breaks off. In ch. 1:18-20 there is yet to come the decision of the judge which shows clearly that the whole is a variant formulation of the JN.

The metaphor in Isa. 5:1-7 describes the court proceeding between God and his people with special vitality and immediacy.[22] Here it is even more clear that when the prophetic judgment-speech is formulated as a judicial procedure, it means the same thing as it does generally. In Micah 6:1-5, after a long introduction of the legal procedure in vs. 1 and 2, there is only the question in vs. 3-5 about the legal basis. This presupposes the apostasy of the nation and contrasts it to the saving acts of Yahweh in a way similar to Jer., ch. 2.

A striking characteristic of this form of the legal procedure lies in the fact that the accusation, in every case, is comprehensive. Each time it is concerned with the whole state of the nation before God. This makes it more understandable that this form of the judicial procedure first received its broadest and most effective expression in Deutero-Isaiah. There it concerns a legal procedure between God and his people which goes back to encompass their whole history. A thoroughgoing and comprehensive treatment of this form would thus have to take the texts in Deutero-Isaiah into consideration.[22a]

2. *The Disputation* (Streitgespräch). The definitive expression of this is also found in Deutero-Isaiah (Begrich, *op. cit.*, pp. 42 ff.). There are many points of contact with the judicial procedure; in Deutero-Isaiah the former often comes first and one frequently cannot make an absolute distinction between them. Micah 2:6-11 and Isa. 28:23-29 are both clearly disputations. The partners in both speeches are not God and his people but the prophet and his opponent. In Micah 2:6-11, Micah's opponents want to hinder his preaching and to deny that he is speaking the word of God (vs. 6-7). Then Micah makes his accusation against them (v. 10). The form of the disputation allows a polemical word against the salvation prophets as an expansion (v. 11). Here, therefore, the disputation has come into a close relationship with the JN.

It is a completely different matter in Isa. 28:23-29! This speech is not intended to be a messenger's speech since Isaiah expressly introduces it as his own word: " Hear my voice." This is the only place in Isa., chs. 1 to 39, where this happens. Here Isaiah consciously speaks with his opponents on their level and seeks to clarify the issue they have contested by using the parable of the farmers. This disputation is important for understanding the different ways the prophetic speech can be formulated in Isaiah because it shows that Isaiah indicates it when a speech does not belong to his message.

In Jeremiah a number of disputations are found. In each case the partners are Yahweh and his nation. Chapter 3:1-5 especially shows how all parts of the JN are woven into the disputation. Other passages are: chs. 2:23-25; 2:29 f., 34 f.; 8:8-9. In Amos, Balla so terms chs. 3:2; 3:12; 5:18-20; 5:24 f.

3. *The Parable.* In the parable in Isa. 5:1-7 the JN in all its parts can be recognized beneath its present wording. The parable serves here — exactly as in the parable of Nathan in II Sam., ch. 12 — to induce the other party to assent to the verdict of God. There are hardly any other

such complete parabolic narratives as Isa. 5:1-7 in the prophecy of the eighth and seventh centuries — a passage like Jer. 13:12-14 might be mentioned. Probably they played a much greater role in the early days of prophecy. Now one finds instead a great number of metaphorical and parabolic expressions that are probably abbreviated parables. Another question to be asked is how the parabolic actions are related to the parabolic narratives. The parabolic action in Jer. 18:1-12 could well be closely related. Its core is the announcement (v. 11b) corresponding to the metaphor in vs. 3-4; the reason is given in the metaphor — the ill-made vessel that must be thrown away. This parabolic action contains therefore all the elements of the judgment-speech. Other parabolic actions are: Isa. 8:1-4; Jer., chs. 19; 16:1-12; Hos., chs. 1 and 3; Ezek. 4:1-3; and others.

4. *The Lament.* The classical death-lament over Israel in Amos 5:1-3 is another way of formulating an announcement of judgment which powerfully depicts the moment of the irrevocable when judgment is proclaimed over Israel. It is also an example of the fact that, under certain circumstances, an announcement can be the prophet's own word without a trace of a reason. Besides Amos 5:1-3, Jer. 9:16-21 also has poetical beauty. In Jeremiah the motif of the lament is more strongly and diversely developed than in any other prophet; besides the lament over Israel (chs. 2:31 f.; 8:4-7, 18-23; 9:9; 10:19 f.; 13:18 f.; 13:23), the lament of Yahweh over his land (chs. 2:31 f.; 12:7-13; 15:5-9; 18:13-17) and the lamentations of Jeremiah (between chs. 11 and 20) are especially well developed.

The lament of Yahweh is already found in Isa. 1:2-3. It is formulated as an accusation against his people: " They have rebelled against me." (Jer. 2:31 f. is quite similar.) It is difficult to decide whether it is meant to be the lament of a father over his faithless child or, because of the " summons to the witnesses " in v. 2, the bringing of a complaint before a court, i.e., before the forum of heaven and earth. It is impossible to distinguish sharply between these. This also shows how near the judicial complaint and the utterly personal lament can come to each other! In a way similar to ch. 1:2-3 an accusation against faithless Jerusalem in ch. 1:21-23 is composed as a lament: "How the faithful city has become a harlot . . .!" Following this is the announcement of judgment that is introduced with the messenger formula (vs. 24-26). In Jer. 2:14-19 (without v. 18) the announcement (vs. 14-16) has the form of a lament. The same is true in Isa. 1:4-9, where the announcement of judgment is formulated as a lament, in ch. 32:9-14, where it resembles the death-lament, and in ch. 22:1-5 (v. 4). The lament in Micah 1:8-16, too, is an announcement of judgment in a different form. In Hos., ch. 7, also in ch. 4:4 ff., and often in Jeremiah, the motifs of the lament are intermingled so that no one part can be clearly identified as a lament. Here, as well, no one has yet made a comprehensive investigation of the lament motifs in prophecy and in their previous history. When, e.g., in the lamentations of Isaiah the addressee is always Jerusalem (also Micah, ch. 1), it can be assumed that an old independent form stands behind these — the lament over a city, features of which still can be seen in other places in the Old Testament (Lamentations).[23]

5. *The Prophetic Torah.*[24] Isa. 1:10-17, 8:11-15, and Jer. 7:21 presuppose a Priestly Torah that contains reproof and instruction in one speech (cf. Gunkel-Begrich, *Einleitungen in die Psalmen,* 1933, pp. 237 f.: "Examples of this form of the Torah with its 'thou shalt' and 'thou shalt not' are offered by Ex. 12:46; Lev. 11:4, 8, 11 . . ."; he then says that the prophets liked to use this form and cites as an example Amos 5:21-24). In Isa. 1:10-17 the summons to hear (v. 10) introduces the reproof (vs. 11-15b); following this is the instruction in vs. 16-17. In between stands a sentence (v. 15c) that does not belong to either but is an accusation: "Your hands are full of blood." This sentence

stands in the middle of the whole. Here, the Torah is divided by the specific prophetic accusation. The announcement of judgment is intimated in v. 15a and b: God will see and hear no longer.

In ch. 8:11-15 the Torah, consisting of reproof (v. 12) and instruction (v. 13), stands in the place of the reason. Then comes the announcement in vs. 14 f., consisting of the intervention of God (v. 14) and its effects (v. 15). Amos, ch. 5, corresponds to Isa., ch. 1; Micah 6:6-8 is a Torahlike question and answer; but there is no relation at all here to the prophetic judgment-speech.

Finally, it can be said in regard to these borrowed speech forms that this partial survey has shown that one cannot place them alongside the others as one possible form of expression for prophetic speech, as has been done many times since Gunkel. They stand in a close relationship with the prophetic judgment-speech. The basic form of the JN is still operative in these variant formulations of the prophetic speech.

VI. THE ANNOUNCEMENT OF JUDGMENT TO ISRAEL'S ENEMIES

One further matter that must be mentioned is that the judgment-speech against other nations is found in the prophets of the eighth and seventh centuries. In part it corresponds exactly to the judgment-speech against the nation of Israel. Such is the case in Amos, chs. 1 and 2, in Isa., chs. 7 and 8; 10:5-15, 24-27, and in the groups of oracles against the foreign nations.[25] This large and complicated body of oracles against foreign nations must be bracketed out here; such a speech is only occasionally employed where there is an obvious formal agreement with the judgment-speech to Israel (as in Amos, chs. 1 and 2). Even where there is for-
204

mal agreement they do not belong in the line of those prophetic speeches examined here in regard to their content. Rather, they belong in the line of salvation-speeches because they imply salvation for Israel in the light of the situation in which they were uttered. That becomes particularly clear in Isa., chs. 7 and 8, where, e.g., the judgment-speech about Aram and (northern) Israel in ch. 7:5-8 is intended to be a salvation-speech to Ahaz. In Isa., chs. 7 and 8, as in Amos, chs. 1 and 2, it can be safely assumed that for both prophets there had been an early period of salvation prophecy [26] which then suddenly changed into judgment prophecy. When oracles against foreign nations which correspond structurally to the JN are found in the judgment prophets, one must ask whether the resemblance is due to some kind of later alteration. It can be assumed that the oracles against foreign nations from the early period had their own distinctive form in the context of salvation prophecy. They were probably not announcements of judgment but of ill fortune (*Unheilsankündigungen*), i.e., it was not necessary for a reason to be given with them; or if there was, it was of a completely different kind. This can only be clarified, however, by an investigation of the whole body of oracles against foreign nations.

VII. THE DISSOLUTION OF THE FORM

The prophetic judgment-speech that is directed to Israel had its season. In the exile the judgment announced by the prophets came true and the historical mission of this form was thus fulfilled. Nowhere can this be seen more clearly than in Deutero-Isaiah. In his proclamation the JN simply does not exist any longer.

Subsequent to the exile, however, the aftereffects can be seen. Haggai and Zechariah are not messengers of the judgment of God as were the prophets of the eighth and seventh centuries, but would belong more appropriately in the line of salvation prophecy. Even then, however, the speech form of the JN was impressed so deeply into the tradition that it can still be recognized, though of course only in an indistinct form. This can be shown with an example (Zech. 1:1-4):

1: In the . . . the word of the Lord came to Zechariah . . . saying,
2: "The Lord was very angry with your fathers.
3: Therefore say to them, Thus says the Lord of hosts: Return to me, says the Lord of hosts, and I will return to you, says the Lord of hosts.
4: Be not like your fathers, to whom the former prophets cried out, 'Thus says the Lord of hosts, Return from your evil ways and from your evil deeds.' But they did not hear or heed me, says the Lord."

The announcement of judgment has been replaced by the call to repentance which incorporates the accusation (". . . from your evil ways"); a conditional announcement of salvation now appears with it in place of the unconditional announcement of judgment. Preexilic prophecy is interpreted accordingly — its proclamation is construed as a call to repentance. The dissolution of the real prophetic judgment-speech in this text can be perceived in a glance. As a matter of fact, so far as we know, there were no more unconditional announcements of judgment from the time of the exile on. It did not return until the proclamation of Jesus in the woes over the cities of Chorazin, Bethsaida, and Capernaum (Matt. 11:20-24; Luke 10:13-15), and the announcement of the fall of the city of Jerusalem in Luke, ch. 11.

The dissolution of the basic form of the prophetic judgment-speech can be seen next in the prose version of individual speeches of Jeremiah in the strata of tradition which Mowinckel calls the C-strata.[27] A good example is Jer. 25:1-13 at the conclusion of the collection contained in chs. 1 to

25. Here the structure of the basic form can still be clearly recognized:

> 1-2: Introduction
> 3-7: Reason (a summarizing accusation)
> 8a: Messenger formula
> 8b-11, 13: Announcement of judgment

The dissolution is to be seen, however, in that the reason is no longer a single, concrete accusation, but describes the reaction of the people not only to the whole work of Jeremiah but also to the work of the prophets before him (Jer. 25:3-13):

> 3: "For twenty-three years, from . . . to . . . , I have spoken persistently to you, but you have not listened.
> 4: . . . although the Lord persistently sent to you all his servants the prophets,
> 5: saying, 'turn now . . . , and dwell upon the land . . . ;
> 6: do not go after other gods. . . .'
> 7: Yet you have not listened to me. . . ."
> 8-13: Announcement of judgment: "Therefore, thus says the Lord of hosts:
> 8b: Because you have not obeyed my words,
> 9: Intervention of God: behold, I will send. . . .
> 10-13: Effect: This whole land shall become a ruin and a waste . . ." (v. 12 excepted).

Here, the announcement of judgment remains essentially the same, but the typical Deuteronomistic description of the prophetic era has appeared in place of the reason. This means that the prophetic proclamation is no longer formed as a concrete accusation, but rather, as a call to repentance, and in fact (v. 5) a call to repentance that is based on a conditional announcement of salvation. We find exactly the same thing in the chronistic stylization of the prophetic speeches.[28]

In Ezekiel the form is dissolved even farther. In ch. 6:1-10, for example, the messenger's speech begins in v. 3 as an announcement of judgment and continues as such all the way to the conclusion. The reason is included by implication in individual sentences and parts of sentences. The whole of ch. 7 is also an announcement of judgment with the reason standing out clearly in only one place — v. 23.

The following is an example of a prophetic speech in Ezekiel (ch. 5) :

1-4: Commission to perform a symbolic act:
And you, O son of man, take a sharp sword.
5-6: Interpretation of the symbolic act: Accusation against Jerusalem
7-17: Announcement of judgment, introduced by a messenger formula (7a)
7b: The reason repeated and summarized: Because you . . .
8-9: Messenger formula, intervention of God: Behold, I, even I . . . ; will . . . .
10: Effect: " fathers shall eat their sons . . ."
and intervention of God
11: Messenger formula, reason, intervention of God.
12-13: Effect, concluding with the knowledge formula (*Erkenntnisformel*)
14-17: Intervention of God and the effects intermingled, description of the judgment.

So even here in the midst of this baroque extravagance where repetition and cumulation have so greatly advanced the dissolution, the basic structure can still be recognized. Even the polarity of accusation and announcement is retained.

A very late stylized imitation of a prophetic judgment-speech is found in Chronicles (II Chron. 15:1-7) . We have already discussed these prophetic speeches. An attempt was made to show that more genuine old prophecy has been preserved there than was previously believed. But otherwise prophetic speeches are found there in which absolutely nothing of the old basic form can be recognized.

208

1: The spirit of God came upon Azariah the son of Oded,
2: and he went out to meet Asa, and said to him,
"Hear me, Asa, and all Judah and Benjamin:
The Lord is with you, while you are with him.
If you seek him, he will be found by you,
but if you forsake him, he will forsake you."
3-6: Description of the past history
7: But you, take courage! Do not let your hands be weak,
for your work shall be rewarded.

A conditional announcement of salvation and judgment
has appeared in place of the unconditional accusation and
the unconditional judgment-speech. The whole is a very
clear expression of the principle of retribution which is
believed by the Chronicler to determine history. Here one
can only speak of a complete dissolution of the old form.

Notes

A. The History of the Investigation

1. H. Birkeland, *Zum hebräischen Traditionswesen: Die Komposition der prophetischen Bücher des AT* (1938) ; J. Engnell, *Profetia och tradition* (Svensk Exeg. Arsb., 1947), pp. 110–139; S. Mowinckel, *Prophecy and Tradition* (1946) ; G. Widengren, *Literary and Psychological Aspects of the Hebrew Prophets* (1948) ; A. R. Johnson, *The Cultic Prophet in Ancient Israel* (1944) ; A. Haldar, *Associations of Cult Prophets Among the Ancient Semites* (1945) ; A. H. J. Gunneweg, *Mündliche und schriftliche Tradition der vorexilischen Prophetenbücher* (Göttingen, 1959).

2. Compare to this the valuable investigation of H. W. Wolff, " Das Thema ' Umkehr' in der alttestamentlichen Prophetie," *Zeitschrift für Theologie und Kirche* (1951), pp. 129–148.

3. First, S. Mowinckel, *Die Komposition des Jeremiabuches* (1914); then, e.g., Rudolph, *Kommentar;* J. Bright, " The Date of the Prose-Sermons of Jeremiah," *Journal of Biblical Literature,* 70 (1951), pp. 15 ff.; and J. W. Miller, *Das Verhältnis Jeremias und Ezechiels untersucht* . . . (1955).

4. J. Hempel, " Die israelitischen Anschauungen von Segen und Fluch im Lichte altorientalischer Parallelen," *Zeitschrift der deutschen Morgenländischen Gesellschaft,* NF 4 (1925), pp. 20–110; J. Scharbert, *Solidarität in Segen und Fluch im AT und in seiner Umwelt* (Bonn, 1958), see further literature there; cf. D. Vetter, *Untersuchungen zum Seherspruch im Alten Testament,* Diss., Heidelberg, 1962.

5. Thus, e.g., in the article in *RGG* [2] by Gunkel, which will be treated below.

6. Steuernagel, *Einleitung*, p. 463, commenting directly upon the sentences cited above.

7. In order to bring this thesis, which is his real starting point, into harmony with the title, Gunkel understands the original literary work of the prophets to be the composition of very short handbills with single short sayings. Widengren has taken up this idea once again, *op. cit.*, p. 121.

8. Cf. the list given by R. B. Y. Scott, *The Relevance of the Prophets* (New York, 1947), p. 100; A. Bentzen, *Introduction*, p. 110.

9. Cf. Steuernagel, above.

10. Compare to this, however, the careful and well-considered remarks by H. W. Wolff about these Egyptian oracles: " Hauptprobleme alttestamentlicher Prophetie," *Evangelische Theologie* (1955), pp. 446–468, 451: " No genuine prophecy is present here, but rather *ex eventu* prediction." In addition, G. Lančzkowski, " Ägyptischer Prophetismus im Lichte des alttestamentlichen," *Zeitschrift für die alttestamentliche Wissenschaft* (1958), pp. 31 ff.

10a. Otherwise Bentzen, *Introduction*, p. 197: " The probability must, however, be taken into consideration, that these formulas (as ' Thus says the Lord ') are common to both Priestly and prophetic oracles . . . But they certainly, as formulae, are elements of ritual language." But that is mere conjecture. It must be shown in clear Priestly speech forms, and this proof cannot be produced in any case from the Old Testament. Bentzen seems convinced of this when he says on p. 194 that the Mari letters show the noncultic character of prophecy.

11. I mean that this is the reason that too much also remains unsatisfactory in Gunkel's definition of prophetic speech forms.

12. One might observe that if this is correct, Gunkel's characterization of the threatening speech in his lexicon article does not hold true at all for the threat, but rather for this other genre which here Balla calls a " judgment-oracle " (*Unheilsorakel*).

13. A. Jepsen, *Nabi* (1934); H. Junker, *Prophet und Seher in Israel* (1927); A. S. Peake, " The Roots of Hebrew Proph-

212

ecy," *Bul JRL* (1927 f.) ; A. Guillaume, *Prophecy and Divination Among the Hebrews and Other Semites* (1938) ; M. Buber, *Sehertum* (Cologne, 1955) .

14. For the sake of terminology, it should be noted that Wolff retains the term *Drohung* or *Drohwort* for the announcement of judgment. The term *Scheltwort* is consistently omitted. Still he can also say in a summary just at the end of his work (p. 20) : " The prophet is mediator between God and man. He comes to his people as God's messenger in order to announce his judgment and salvation."

15. French and English equivalents were formed. Cf. the work of Scott (see above) and A. Néher, *L'Essence du Prophétisme* (Paris, 1955) .

16. In referring to the summaries by Eissfeldt and Weiser in their introductions, G. Fohrer says in his literature survey, " Neuere Literatur zur alttestamentlichen Prophetie," *Theologische Rundschau* (1951 and 1952) , Part 1, " Literatur von 1932–39," p. 336: " The short, often summary, list reveals that we are still a long way from an adequate comprehension and illumination of the various prophetic genres."

17. See also O. Grether, " Name und Wort Gottes im AT," *Beihefte zur Zeitschrift für die alttestamentliche Wissenschaft* (1934, 64) . That which Grether determines here to be the meaning of *dābār* is true of an announcement of judgment, but not of a threat.

18. Both of the terms which I used here originated in an old tradition; used similarly by Hitzig, *Jesajakommentar*, p. 80; Duhm entitles his nineteenth section " Begründung der Unheilsankündigung " (*Israels Propheten*, 1916) and begins by explaining these terms; by Steuernagel in the above quotation, and by many others.

19. Cf. Westermann, " Struktur und Geschichte der Klage im AT," *ZAW* 66, 1–2 (Berlin, 1954) .

20. Cf. J. Begrich, " Deuterojesajastudien," *Beiträge zum Wissenschaft von Alten Testament*, 4, F.H. 25 (1938/39) .

20a. Also similar are N. W. Porteous, " Prophecy," *Record and Revelation* (Oxford, 1938) , pp. 216–249; G. H. Davies, " The Jahwistic Tradition in the Eighth Century Prophets," *Studies in Old Testament Prophecy* (Edinburgh, 1950); E. Rohland, *Die Bedeutung der Erwählungstraditionen Israels für die Eschatologie der AT-lichen Propheten* (diss., Heidelberg, 1956).

21. Cf. the other, unacceptable reason for the coexistence of salvation prophecy and judgment prophecy in Gressmann.

21a. This is said exactly or similarly by Balla, *op. cit.*, par. 11b; Hempel, *op. cit.*, p. 60; Scott, *op. cit.*, p. 179; H. W. Wolff, *ZAW* (1934), p. 6; *Das Zitat im Prophetenspruch*, p. 71.

22. This relationship becomes even clearer in an expansion of prophetic judgment-speeches found throughout the prophecy of the eighth and seventh centuries. More will be said concerning this later.

23. E.g., the sentence on p. 33, "The visions show how the *nābī'*, Amos, is separated step by step from the essential functions of his office."

24. "Proclamation of individual sayings, commands, threats, or promises that had meaning for special situations." (Baudissin, *op. cit.*, p. 312, continued by Gunkel.)

B. A Survey

1. Wisdom speeches are also found in the prophetic books. They are omitted here only for the sake of clarity.

2. O. Grether, "Name und Wort Gottes im AT," *BZAW* (1934), p. 64.

2a. The following investigation is limited to the prophetic judgment-speech. For the salvation-speech, cf. C. Westermann, "The Way of the Promise Through the Old Testament," *The Old Testament and Christian Faith*, ed. by B. W. Anderson (New York, 1963), pp. 200–224.

3. The concepts "prophet" and "prophecy" extend beyond this time in both directions, but that does not change the statement above at all.

4. That is confirmed by Ezek., chs. 40 to 48. One such program is found in a prophetic book for the first time *after* the collapse of the kingship and preexilic temple cult.

5. An early form of prophecy in the Northern Kingdom, which is described in the Elijah-Elisha stories, is an exception.

6. Characteristically the tradition of Solomon forms an exception here. Many times a speech of God comes directly to

him; on the other hand, no prophetic activity is seen during his reign.

7. As especially in the early period of David.

8. Primarily by L. Köhler, J. Lindblom, H. W. Wolff, and H. Wildberger.

9. Cf. the article, " Euangelion," by Schniewind in *Theologisches Wörterbuch zum Neuen Testament*.

10. *Archives royales de Mari*, Bd. I–VIII (The Louvre, Paris) ; W. von Soden, " Verkündigung des Gotteswillens durch prophetisches Wort in altbabylonische Briefen aus Mari," *Welt des Orients* I, Heft 15 (Aug., 1950) , pp. 397–403; —— " Das altbabylonische Briefarchiv von Mari," *Welt des Orients* (1948) , 3, pp. 187 ff.; (further literature is found there) ; M. Noth, " Geschichte und Gotteswort im AT," *Gesammelte studien zum AT* (1957) , pp. 230 ff.; H. Schmökel, " Gotteswort in Mari und Israel," *Theologische Literaturzeitung* (1951) , cols. 53–59; A. Néher, *L'Essence du Prophetisme* (Paris, 1955) , pp. 23–29; N. H. Ridderboes, *Israels Profetie en 'profetie' buiten Israel* (The Hague, 1955) ; E. Weidner, " Babylonische Prophezeiungen," *Archiv für Orientforschung* (1939/41) ; A. Lods and G. Dossin, " Une Tablette inédite de Mari . . . ," *Studies in Old Testament Prophecy,* ed. by T. H. Robinson (Edinburgh, 1950) , pp. 103 f.

11. Cf. G. von Rad, *Der heilige Krieg im alten Israel* (Göttingen, 1952) , pp. 6 ff.

12. In regard to the self-predication of God in the messenger's speech see A. Bentzen, *Introduction,* p. 187.

13. E.g., G. Quell, *Wahre und falshe Propheten* (Gütersloh, 1952) .

C. The Prophetic Judgment-Speech to Individuals

1. Regarding the text of I Kings 21:18-19, it should be noted that the introduction formulas in the tradition of the text are quite uncertain. It is highly improbable that the messenger formula occurred (MS) twice in such a short and early speech. The first, " *so sprach Jahwe* " in v. 19a must be canceled.

2. Here it is joined to the speech as a participle: " Now hear the word of the Lord, you who say . . ." (*M.T.*) . This con-

struction reveals that the summons to hear is directly related to the announcement. The reason is only in apposition to the address.

3. This is not the case in Amos, ch. 7. Here no one intervenes because the action of the priest Amaziah is judged by the public to be justified and not punishable. However, kingly authority also stands behind it. Amaziah does not act against any principle of the old law of God; to be sure, however, he prevents the old law of God from being heard from the mouth of Amos.

4. " Das Zitat im Prophetenspruch," *ZAW* (1934). Smend (*Theologische Studien und Kritiken*, 4, p. 611) has already seen that the prophets presuppose a legal tradition.

5. H. W. Wolff, *Hosea* ("Biblische Kommentar"), ch. 4:1-3: " As the situation in life of *rib* one will sooner accept the proclamation of judgment by the legal community which deliberated at the city gates." J. Begrich is in agreement with this, " Studien zu Deuterojesaja," *BWANT*, IV, 25 (1928), pp. 19–41. Opposing is E. Würthwein, *ZThK*, 49 (1952), pp. 1 ff. Cf. H. E. von Waldow, *Anlass und Hintergrund der Verkündigung Deuterojesajas* (diss., Bonn, 1953), pp. 37 ff. Also opposed to Würthwein's thesis is F. Hesse, " Wurzelt die prophetische Gerichtsrede im israelitischen Kult? " *ZAW* (1953), pp. 45–53. Würthwein's thesis agrees with A. H. J. Gunneweg, *op. cit.* (Part A, note 1), p. 98. The sentence by H. W. Wolff cited above is significantly supported by the investigation by H. J. Boecker, *Redeformen des israelitischen Rechtslebens* (diss., Bonn, 1959), pp. 75 ff.

5a. Balla, par. 10: Amos differs from all of his predecessors in that he saw total destruction coming for Israel (previously it was for the enemies or an individual, e.g., the king).

5b. A characteristic aftereffect of the JI is found in Jer. 2:18, 36-37, and 2:33. Both are judgment-speeches against Israel, but are in the style of JI.

6. The announcement of judgment against Zedekiah in Ezek. 17:11-21 has been considerably altered but still contains elements of the old JI; on the other hand, Ezek. 11:13 (Pelatiah) has the characteristics of a curse.

7. It is possible that Jer. 22:15, the second generalizing sentence, was inserted later.

216

8. In I Sam. 15:23 the accusation is once more included in a causal sentence. That holds true for what was said above concerning II Sam. 12:9a. The passage shows that the grammatical connection between both parts belongs to a secondary stage.

9. Cf. C. Westermann, " Struktur und Geschichte der Klage im AT," *ZAW*, 66, 1/2 (1954).

9a. Cf. H. J. Boecker's dissertation given in note 5 of this section.

10. See also F. Hesse, *op. cit.*, pp. 45–53; p. 50.

D. The Announcement of Judgment Against Israel

1. This was already seen by Graf Baudissin (*op. cit.*, p. 316) : " Judging from the established forms of rhetoric found in the prophets of this century, such speech as this had already been in existence a long time before "; and in Balla as well, par. 10; and Hempel, p. 66: " The origin of the more developed genres is even before Amos. Amos is not the beginning, but already a point of culmination." Cf. also Bentzen, *Introduction*, p. 160.

2. Here it can only be pointed out that there are still completely different contexts that are to be considered in regard to this earlier history. To be sure, they belong more in the line of salvation prophecy, because they are words of judgment against non-Israelites. The first to be mentioned is Gen. 19:13:

> For we are about to destroy this place,
> because the outcry against its people has become great before the Lord,
> and the Lord has sent us to destroy it.

In spite of all the disparity, an announcement with a reason can still be clearly recognized. The primary difference is that the persons who make the announcements are at the same time those who execute the judgment.

Above all, however, the whole complex of the announcement of plagues in Egypt belongs here; on this point compare the dissertation by F. Schnutenhaus, *Die Entstehung der Mosetraditionen* (Heidelberg, 1958), pp. 27 ff.: the plague stories. We can take for an example, Ex. 7:15 ff.:

Go to Pharaoh. . . . And you shall say to him,
" The Lord, the God of the Hebrews, sent me to you,
saying, ' Let my people go, that they may serve me in the
wilderness; and behold, you have not yet obeyed.'
Thus says the Lord, '. . . I will strike the water that is
in the Nile.' "

This passage is very similar to the delivery of a message in
the profane realm; it is quite possible that an early form of the
prophetic announcement is present here, but it is more in
the line of salvation prophecy. A further example that
strengthens this thesis comes in Ex. 4:21-23:

And the Lord said to Moses,
" When you go back to Egypt . . . .
And you shall say to Pharaoh,
' Thus says the Lord,
Israel is my first-born son,
and I say to you, " Let my son go that he may serve me ";
if you refuse to let him go,
behold, I will slay your first-born son.' "

Even if this is a question of a secondary formulation (see
M. Noth concerning this), its stylization in the manner of a
profane messenger's speech is striking. The indicative and imperative part of the message can be recognized clearly (cf. Gen.
45:9; Num. 22:13 ff.) ; both of the last lines resemble the message of Jephthah in Judges, ch. 11, which likewise terminates
in an announcement. Undoubtedly there are connections here;
a comprehensive investigation of these messages is urgently
needed.

3. Cf. R. B. Y. Scott and H. W. Wolff.

4. A great number of prophetic speeches are related to this
interval of time, e.g., Isa. 5:18 f.

5. H. W. Wolff speaks of a " normal form," *ZAW* (1934),
pp. 2 ff.

6. I see a confirmation of the two-part nature of the announcement of judgment in the story of the call of Jeremiah
(Jer., ch. 1) . The basic elements of the prophecy are found in
the middle: in v. 7b the command to be a messenger, and in
the metaphors in v. 10b, the commission to announce judg-

ment and salvation. Both aspects of the announcement of judgment are developed again in the two visions in vs. 11-15: the "watching branch" with the interpretation "I am watching over my word" points to the intervention of God; the boiling pot with the interpretation "Out of the north evil shall break forth" points to the results of this intervention.

6a. The formation of series such as Amos, chs. 1 and 2; Isa. 9:7-20 with 5:25-29; and the series of woes as Isa. 5:8-24 and 10:1-4 (see below) is not one of the variations. To the contrary, they are certainly a particularly clear witness to the fact that the judgment-speech had its own well-established structure; they are certainly to be seen, at least in part, as the oldest collections of prophetic speeches. The compelling power of this structure can be seen in Amos, chs. 1 and 2, in that the later imitations have adopted it. From another viewpoint, these series constructions beautifully illustrate the freedom that was exercised in the formation of the speeches; it is clear that in Amos, chs. 1 and 2, the announcement must be the more stereotyped part. In spite of that, the individual speeches here vary, for in a few, God only announces his intervention and in others the effect still follows it.

7. *Einleitung in die Psalmen* (1933).

8. That the part which has become independent itself tacitly presupposes the other part can be shown best in an example of a JI. In the speech of Jeremiah to the priest, Passhur (Jer. 20:1-6), the announcement stands (v. 3) without a reason. That is possible here because it becomes so clear from the preceding narrative that it need not be expressed.

9. E.g., Isa. 8:5-8; 29:13-14; 30:12-14. Cf. H. W. Wolff, *op. cit., ZAW* (1934), p. 5: "Only Isaiah and Jeremiah have this reason in a causal sentence in type b-a and both are introduced by ya'an. Only Isaiah begins with ya'an kî, and only Jeremiah with ya'an 'ašer. These causal connections show the literary character of such constructions."

10. The contrast motif in the complaint of the people is similar to this. In it the same motif is encountered — a retrospective view of the earlier saving acts of God. There, however, it is made from a completely different viewpoint. The contrast is not with the wickedness but with the suffering of the present generation (Ps. 80; 44; 89). Just as in the prophetic

219

speech, they are stimulated to look at their connections with the past when they discover the contrasts between the earlier saving act of God as it has been passed down in the confession and the present which stands in contradiction to it. In this case there is the inconceivable contradiction of the blow that fell upon the people (Ps. 89:2 ff. and 39 ff.), and in the other, that of the inconceivable reaction of the people (Isa. 5:2 and 7). Both contrast motifs show how a lively, sensitive historical consciousness arose among these people. Sometime they should be investigated together and compared.

10a. Foreign influences are possible in this enlargement into a description of annihilation; cf. Néher's Egyptian examples, *op. cit.*, pp. 21 ff.

11. Cf. Wildberger's investigation.

12. Balla had already seen this; see also Lindblom, p. 100.

13. Cf. Grether, *op. cit.*, concerning $n^{e'}um\ yhwh$. Lindblom, *op. cit.*, pp. 66 f., says, " The formula *'āmar yhwh* first came into use in the language of Deutero-Isaiah or the postexilic period, while on the other hand, the formula $n^{e'}um\ yhwh$ probably just came to be used as a prophetic style rather late."

14. In regard to this entire section, see Lindblom, *op. cit.*, supplement, " Die prophetische Orakelformel."

15. Cf. Zimmerli, *Ezekiel* (" Biblische Kommentar zum AT ").

16. Lindblom believes that in Isa. 5:7, *hôy* should stand at the beginning as was proposed (Smith) and says concerning chs. 5:8 ff.; 5:18; and 6:1, " This gives us a series of 3 woe-revelations." Also V. Maag, *Text, Wortschatz und Begriffswelt des Propheten Amos* (Leiden, 1951).

17. G. v. d. Leeuw, *Phänomenologie der Religion* (1933), p. 464.

17a. Hölscher has already pointed out the relation with the tribal aphorisms in Gen., ch. 49, and Deut., ch. 33. Cf. H. J. Kittel, "Sprüche mit der Struktur des Prophetenspruches," *Die Stammessprüche Israels* (diss., Berlin, 1959), pp. 91–95. A. Bentzen, " The Ritual Background of Amos 1-2," *Old Testament Studies*, VII (1950), pp. 85–99, sees a relation of the oracles against foreign nations (esp. Amos, chs. 1 and 2) with curses that were spoken in the cultic service over enemy groups (nations), parallel to the Egyptian execration texts.

18. Also behind the aphorism about Reuben, Gen. 49:3-4 is a curse, which, however, is no longer recognizable at all.

19. So also A. Alt, Vol. II, p. 314.

19a. K. Baltzer, " Das Bundesformular " (diss., 1957, p. 20, *Wissenschaftliche Beiträge zum Alten Testament*, 3, Neukirchen, 1960).

20. P. Humbert, "Die Herausforderungsformel *hinnēnî ēlékā*," *ZAW*, 51 (1933), pp. 101–108.

21. H. W. Wolff, " Muster eines prophetischen Gerichtwortes."

22. Würthwein, *op. cit.*, p. 4, does not always state the entire prophetic speech, but only the verses containing the picture of the judicial proceedings. He doesn't mention Isa. 1:18-20 and 5:1-7.

22a. Cf. Begrich, *Deuterojesaja-Studien* (1938), pp. 19 ff. Cf. the entire section H. J. Boecker, *op. cit.*, C II, " Die Urteilsfolgebestimmung," pp. 145 ff. Here the origin in the profane judgment-speech is confirmed. For the disputation, see E. Pfeiffer, " Die Disputationsworte im Buch Maleachi," *EvTh* 12 (1959), pp. 546–568.

23. Stählin, " Die Totenklage des Propheten," *TWNT*, Vol. III, pp. 838–840. " Die Totenklage im AT " (*kopetos*), cites also Ezek., chs. 19; 26:15-18; (27; 28:11-19); 32:19-32; 37:32b-34. No position is taken on the form and its history.

24. Cf. Bentzen, *Introduction*, 1952[2], pp. 163, 184 ff., 201.

25. Hempel, *op. cit.*, p. 64, " In its own threats, however, the judgment prophecy itself produced such strong literary forms that salvation-oracles for Israel were worded in the form of threats of doom (against the foreign peoples) (Hos. 5:12 ff.; 13:7 f.) ."

26. Cf. Würthwein.

27. *Zur Komposition des Buches Jeremia* (Kristiana, 1914), adopted along with others by Rudolph in his commentary.

28. The same can be found in the temple speech (Jer. 7:1-15), which is also transmitted in the Deuteronomic version behind which the original prophetic speech can still be clearly recognized. It is found in vs. 4, 9-12, and 14. In the secondary Deuteronomic version the speech v. 3a can begin with a warning and conditional salvation announcement which is broadly

developed in vs. 5-7. In v. 8, v. 4 must now — because of the
wide interval — be again repeated. In v. 13 — just as in ch.
25:8b — the announcement is begun with a summation of the
reason. This is also reminiscent of the wording in ch. 25.